Best Easy Day Hikes
Baltimore

Help Us Keep This Guide Up to Date

Every effort has been made by the author and editors to make this guide as accurate and useful as possible. However, many things can change after a guide is published—trails are rerouted, regulations change, facilities come under new management, and so forth.

We appreciate hearing from you concerning your experiences with this guide and how you feel it could be improved and kept up to date. While we may not be able to respond to all comments and suggestions, we'll take them to heart, and we'll also make certain to share them with the author. Please send your comments and suggestions to the following address:

> GPP
> Reader Response/Editorial Department
> PO Box 480
> Guilford, CT 06437

Or you may e-mail us at:

> editorial@GlobePequot.com

Thanks for your input, and happy trails!

Best Easy Day Hikes Series

Best Easy Day Hikes
Baltimore

Heather Sanders Connellee

FALCONGUIDES

GUILFORD, CONNECTICUT
HELENA, MONTANA

AN IMPRINT OF GLOBE PEQUOT PRESS

This book is dedicated to my grandfathers, Walter Srnec, Sr. (1921–2012) and Elmer Sanders.

To buy books in quantity for corporate use or incentives, call **(800) 962-0973** or e-mail **premiums@GlobePequot.com**.

FALCONGUIDES®

FalconGuides in an imprint of Globe Pequot Press.
Falcon, FalconGuides, and Outfit Your Mind are registered trademarks of Morris Book Publishing, LLC.

Maps: Trailhead Graphics Inc. © Morris Book Publishing, LLC
Project editor: Julie Marsh
Layout: Sue Murray

Library of Congress Cataloging-in-Publication Data is available on file.
ISBN: 978-0-7627-6990-2

Printed in the United States of America

10 9 8 7 6 5 4 3 2 1

The author and Globe Pequot Press assume no liability for accidents happening to, or injuries sustained by, readers who engage in the activities described in this book.

Contents

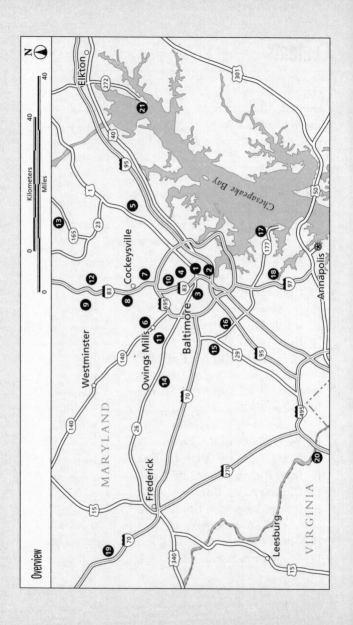

Acknowledgments

First, I'd like to thank the many rangers and park staff who were enthusiastically willing to share information on their parks and trails. I certainly couldn't have done this without them. A big thank-you to all my family and friends who support my love of the outdoors and adventure, regardless of how crazy they may think I am at times. And a shout-out to my hiking partners, Grant, Grace, Paige, and Rachel!

I'd like to extend a giant thank-you to the thousands of volunteers who keep these trails safe and looking spiffy. Few people realize that volunteers are the ones maintaining many of our trails. So don't forget to pay it back! While you're at it, invite a friend or family member to join you on the trail. Expose someone new to the outdoors and pay it forward.

Of course, thank you to my amazing husband, who supported me through this entire process. It's been quite a year—planning our wedding, rehabbing our home, and writing a book. His love and support helped carry us through a very busy year. I couldn't have done it with anyone else. It's been a lot of fun and hard work to make it to the finish! Just like hiking a mountain, the uphill climb is worth every exhausting step once you reach the reward on top.

Introduction

So what can a working-class port town, famous for steamed crabs and Orioles baseball, possibly have to offer in the way of hiking trails? You will be surprised! Baltimore is rich in recreation and history. Yes, it's the birthplace of "The Star-Spangled Banner" and home to Ravens football and the Preakness Stakes. While downtown Baltimore City is made up of concrete sidewalks, row homes, high-rises, boutique shops, and trendy neighborhood restaurants and pubs, there are hidden gems of lush parks and greenways secretly placed among the hustle and bustle, just waiting to be explored. Baltimore County and surrounding counties comprise rolling hills, farmland, and vineyards offering much in the way of circumventing the cement.

The largest city in the state of Maryland, Baltimore is located 100 miles from Philadelphia and 40 miles from Washington, D.C. I agree, hiking isn't the first thing that comes to mind when you think of Baltimore, and it is hard to escape the lingering sound of traffic in the distance, but you'll be amazed at the numerous outdoor opportunities awaiting you in this busy little city. From rail trails to lakes, arboretums, national parks, rivers, a covered bridge, scenic overlooks, three reservoir watersheds, and a lighthouse—many Baltimoreans don't even know most of these places exist. Baltimore is located on a line between the Piedmont Plateau and the Atlantic Coastal Plain, and its number-one natural resource is the Chesapeake Bay watershed. While they may not be as remote as the foothills of the Idaho wilderness or as rugged as the Teton Mountains in Wyoming, Baltimore's trails have character and charm all of their own. Hence Baltimore's nickname—Charm City.

1

Weather

Baltimore's proximity to the Chesapeake Bay, the Atlantic Ocean to the east, and the Appalachian Mountains to the west means a moderate and humid climate with hot summers and mostly mild winters. Spring is warm and mostly dry, with temperatures in the sixties and seventies. On average, July is the hottest and rainiest month of the year, with temperatures in the high eighties to mid-nineties. But the summer heat certainly doesn't end there. It's not unusual for August and even early September to bring those same hot July temperatures. Fall temperatures will dip down into the fifties and sixties. While summer and early fall are thunderstorm and hurricane seasons, fall and spring are still the best times to hike, with cooler temperatures, spring blossoms, and fall foliage. The average annual snowfall in Baltimore is 20 inches. And remember, there is no such thing as bad weather—only bad clothing. So, if you want an enjoyable hike, do your homework, check the weather, wear appropriate clothing, and always be prepared.

Safety and Preparation

While you don't have to be worried about deadly crocodiles or polar bears in the Baltimore hiking vicinity, there are other safety hazards to be aware of. Especially in the summer months, poison ivy, poison oak, and poison sumac grow well in Baltimore's moist, humid climate. Poison ivy is the most common poisonous plant. It grows as a vine or a shrub and typically has three groups of leaves growing off of one stem. The leaves are pointed or almond-shaped and have a somewhat shiny surface. The plant ranges in color, based on the season, from light green and dark green to red, orange, or yellow. Contact with this plant results in an itching, red skin rash. Although annoying, the result generally isn't serious. The rash typically goes away within a few weeks, and treatment includes over-the-counter anti-itch medications.

Ticks are prevalent from early spring to fall and are known to transmit Lyme disease. Wear light-colored clothing so you can easily spot any hitchhikers, and check your clothing and body after your hike. If a tick has gotten under your skin, remove it by using tweezers to grip the tick from behind the head and as close to the skin as you can get. Gently pull it off. Do not smash or burn it. Clean the tick bite with antiseptic.

The copperhead snake is the only venomous snake found in the Baltimore and surrounding counties. It can be identified by its triangular-shaped head and solid copper color, often with an hourglass pattern with dark lines crisscrossing over a lighter background. The snake's colors range from pinkish, tan, and brown to rust. Copperheads are most commonly found in rocky areas. A copperhead bite is seldom fatal.

And a few last tips on safety and preparedness . . .

Wear sturdy shoes to protect your feet and ankles and to keep your feet dry. Several hikes listed in this book do not have public facilities, so be sure to carry extra water and food. Dress in layers, and always tell someone where you are going and when you expect to return. Carrying a cell phone is recommended, but not for casual conversations; it should be used only to call for help in true emergencies. Always be prepared for any situation, and think about packing the items on American Hiking Society's list of ten essentials of hiking (see page 4). Learn more at www.americanhiking.org.

Ten Essentials of Hiking

- Appropriate footwear
- Map and compass/GPS
- Water
- Extra food
- Rain gear and extra layers
- Safety items: fire, light, and whistle
- First-aid kit
- Knife
- Sunscreen/sunglasses
- Daypack

Leave No Trace

Some trails in the Baltimore area and neighboring counties are heavily used year-round, and some have sensitive ecosystems. We, as trail users and advocates, must be especially vigilant to make sure our passage leaves no lasting mark. Here are some basic guidelines for preserving trails in the region:

- Be prepared. Bring or wear clothes to protect you from cold, heat, or rain. Use maps to navigate (and do not rely solely on the maps included in this book).

- Avoid damaging trailside soils and plants by remaining on the established route. This is also a good rule of thumb for avoiding trailside irritants like poison ivy.

- Pack out all your own trash, including biodegradable items like orange peels. You might also pack out garbage left by less considerate hikers. Use outhouses at trailheads or along the trail, and keep water sources clean.

- Don't pick wildflowers or gather rocks, antlers, feathers, and other treasures along the trail. Removing these items will only take away from the next hiker's experience.

- Be careful with fire. Use a camp stove for cooking. Be sure it's okay to build a campfire in the area you're visiting. Use an existing fire ring and keep your fire small. Use sticks from the ground as kindling. Burn all the wood to ash and be sure the fire is completely out and cold before leaving.

- Don't approach or feed any wild creatures—the ground squirrel eyeing your snack food is best able to survive if it remains self-reliant. Control pets at all times.

- Be kind to other visitors. Be courteous by not making loud noises while hiking and be aware that you share the trail with others. Yield to other trail users when appropriate.

For more information visit LNT.org.

How to Use This Guide

This guide is designed to be simple and easy to use. The overview map at the beginning of the book shows the location of each hike by number, keyed to the table of contents. Each hike is accompanied by a route map that shows access roads, the highlighted featured route, and directional arrows to point you in the right direction. It indicates the general outline of the hike. Due to scale restrictions it is not as detailed as a park map might be or even as our "Miles and Directions" are. While most of the hikes are on clearly designated paths, use these route maps in conjunction with other resources.

Each hike begins with summary information that delivers the trail's vital statistics, including length, difficulty, fees and permits, park hours, canine compatibility, and trail contacts. Directions to the trailhead are also provided, along with a general description of what you'll see along the way. A detailed route finder ("Miles and Directions") sets forth mileages between significant landmarks along the trail.

Hike Selection

This guide describes trails that are accessible to every hiker, whether a visitor from out of town or a proud Baltimorean looking to escape the daily grind in search of some green. The hikes are no longer than 6 miles round-trip, and many are considerably shorter. They range in difficulty from flat trails perfect for a family outing to more challenging treks among the rolling hills of Baltimore and surrounding counties. While these trails are among the best, keep in mind that nearby trails, often in the same park or preserve, may offer options better suited to your needs. I've sought to space out the hikes throughout Baltimore City and County and the surrounding area so that wherever you are starting, you'll find a great easy day hike nearby.

Difficulty Ratings

These are all easy hikes, but easy is a relative term. Some would argue that there are no mountains in Baltimore and therefore all hikes must be easy. While the trails are not nearly as rugged as the mountainous terrain of the West, you will still encounter challenges like uphill climbs, rocky terrain, extreme heat, and exposed areas. To aid in the selection of a hike that suits particular needs and abilities, each is rated easy, moderate, or more challenging. Bear in mind that even the most challenging routes can be made easy by hiking within your limits and taking rests when you need them.

- **Easy** hikes are generally short and flat, taking no longer than an hour to complete.
- **Moderate** hikes involve increased distance and relatively mild changes in elevation and will take one to two hours to complete.
- **More challenging** hikes feature some steep stretches, greater distances, and generally take longer than two hours to complete.

These are completely subjective ratings—consider that what you think is easy is entirely dependent on your level of fitness and the adequacy of your gear (primarily shoes). If you are hiking with a group, you should select a hike with a rating that's appropriate for the least fit and prepared in your party.

Hiking times are approximate, based on the assumption that on flat ground, most walkers average 2 miles per hour. Adjust that rate by the steepness of the terrain and your level of fitness (subtract time if you're an aerobic animal and add time if you're hiking with kids), and you have a ballpark hiking duration. Be sure to add more time if you plan to picnic or take part in other activities like bird-watching or photography.

Trail Finder

Best Hikes for Dogs

Best Hikes for Birders

Best Hikes for Urbanites

Best Hikes for Lake Lovers

Best Hikes for Geology Lovers

Map Legend

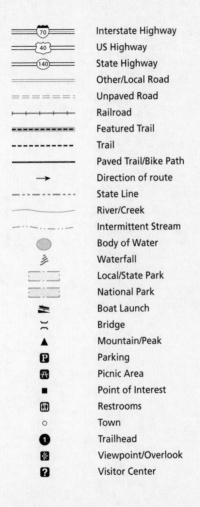	Interstate Highway
	US Highway
	State Highway
	Other/Local Road
	Unpaved Road
	Railroad
	Featured Trail
	Trail
	Paved Trail/Bike Path
	Direction of route
	State Line
	River/Creek
	Intermittent Stream
	Body of Water
	Waterfall
	Local/State Park
	National Park
	Boat Launch
	Bridge
	Mountain/Peak
	Parking
	Picnic Area
	Point of Interest
	Restrooms
	Town
	Trailhead
	Viewpoint/Overlook
	Visitor Center

1 Baltimore Waterfront Promenade: Canton Waterfront Park to Fells Point

An urban hike through the heart of downtown Baltimore's tourist center takes you past restaurants and pubs, boutique shops, attractions, and marinas. Meander through the historic town of Fells Point or continue on the trail to the Inner Harbor, Baltimore's tourist mecca, all while enjoying the view of the water.

Distance: 4.4 miles out and back

Hiking time: About 2 hours

Difficulty: Moderate due to distance

Trail surface: Paved walkway

Best season: Year-round

Other trail users: Runners, bicyclists, skaters

Canine compatibility: Leashed dogs permitted

Fees and permits: None required

Schedule: Promenade always open

Maps: http://waterfrontpartnership .org/waterfront-walking-map

Trail contacts: 650 S. Exeter St., #200, Baltimore; (443) 743-3308; www.waterfrontpartnership.org

Other: Restaurants, cafes, boutique shops are along the way; Baltimore water taxi information and schedule at http:// baltimorewatertaxi.com/

Finding the trailhead: From I-95 take exit 57 for Boston Street. Canton Waterfront Park will be on your left in the 3000 block of Boston Street. A parking lot and street parking are available. GPS: N39 16.626'/W76 34.358'

The Hike

This path is the epitome of urban hiking. Soak in some Baltimore culture while seeing the sights, taking in great

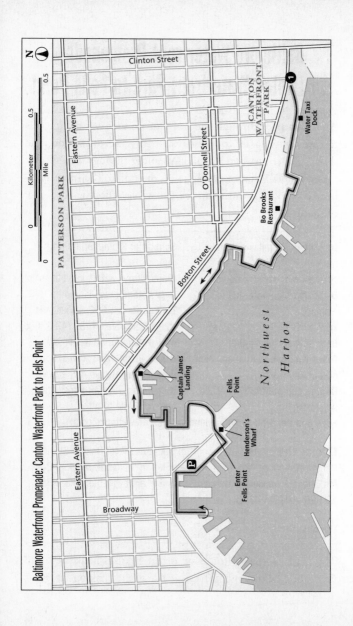

views, and getting some exercise. The entire length of the trail is 7 miles running from Fort McHenry to the Canton Waterfront Park, with some disconnected sections, boardwalk, brick, and sidewalk. This hike describes a well-marked section of the trail from Canton Waterfront Park to the Fells Point pier. Large green signs with the waterfront promenade logo appear along the way. On this section you will pass by several marinas, residences, and restaurants where you can be sure to get a whiff of steamed crabs and fresh seafood. At Canton Waterfront Park you'll often see locals with rod in hand out for a fresh catch of fish or blue crabs. This park is also a popular spot for Baltimoreans to play Frisbee with their dogs or throw down a blanket to sunbathe, picnic, or enjoy a good book.

As you meander along the water's edge, eye up the sailboats and yachts, hear outdoor diners clanking plates and forks, and notice the numerous pubs. Think about stopping in one of the art galleries, gelato or ice-cream shops, or clothing and gift boutiques as you enter the historic neighborhood of Fells Point, famous for its maritime history. Along the cobblestone streets you may see the Urban Pirates ship docked, and then what looks to be an abandoned police station. This structure was used specifically for the filming of the network police drama *Homicide: Life on the Street*.

No doubt, it's an urban trail, so expect to see trash and construction along the way. The floating trash that gathers in some sections of the harbor is quite disturbing. But the positives of this hike most certainly outweigh the negatives. If you choose to continue on the trail past the suggested turnaround at Fells Point, you will eventually circle through the Inner Harbor and past famous attractions such as Harbor Place, the Science Center, and the Aquarium. Fells Point is also a water taxi stop, so you may choose to do your return trip by hopping aboard a taxi back to Canton Waterfront Park.

Miles and Directions

0.0 Begin the trail at Canton Waterfront Park, just steps from the Canton water taxi dock.

0.1 When you are facing the water, go right to follow the brick path.

0.2 Pass by the outdoor dining area of Bay Café restaurant and begin walking along the marina.

0.3 Pass by Bo Brooks restaurant and crab house as you hug the water on your left.

0.5 Pass the pier where you will often see Baltimore's Black-Eyed Susan paddleboat docked.

0.7 Cross a wooden bridge.

1.1 Captain James Landing Restaurant and taxi dock come into view. Follow the trail behind the restaurant and continue on the brick-paved path.

1.2 The trail changes briefly from brick to boardwalk and then concrete.

1.3 Briefly walk through a parking lot and turn left to rejoin the boardwalk.

1.7 Come upon the Inn at Henderson's Wharf. Walk through the parking roundabout to continue on the brick path.

1.8 The trail becomes boardwalk again.

1.9 Enter the neighborhood of Fells Point. Turn left on Thames Street to follow the brick sidewalk.

2.0 Reach the film set for *Homicide: Life on the Street,* what looks to be a police station.

2.1 Come to the Fells Point water taxi dock.

2.2 Follow the path to the end of the pier jutting out into the water. Turn around and retrace your route back to the beginning.

4.4 Arrive back at Canton Waterfront Park.

2 Fort McHenry National Monument and Historic Shrine: Seawall Trail

The American flag waves above as you hike the Seawall Trail, a short path that circles an eighteenth–century star-shaped fort. Birthplace of the national anthem, Fort McHenry is bounded by a perimeter trail that follows along the seawall of Baltimore's harbor, affording expansive views of the city's waterfront and the city skyline and industrial areas.

Distance: 0.8-mile loop
Hiking time: About 30 minutes
Difficulty: Easy
Trail surface: Paved walkway
Best season: Year-round
Other trail users: Bicyclists
Canine compatibility: Dogs permitted on the grounds but not in the historic areas or visitor center. Dogs must be on a leash at all times.
Fees and permits: No fee or permit required to hike the Seawall Trail. Fee for those ages 16 and older to visit the National Monument and Historic Shrine.

Schedule: Park open 8 a.m.–5 p.m., fort and visitor center open 8 a.m.–4:45 p.m. Closed Thanksgiving, Christmas, and New Year's Day.
Maps: No maps available
Trail contacts: 2400 E. Fort Ave., Baltimore; (410) 962-4290; www.nps.gov/fomc/
Other: Fort McHenry can be reached by water taxi; information and schedule can be found at http://baltimorewatertaxi.com/

Finding the trailhead: From I-95 take exit 55 to Key Highway. From Key Highway turn left on Lawrence Street and then left on Fort Avenue. Proceed 1 mile to the park. GPS: N39 15.907'/W76 34.787'

The Hike

Located in Federal Hill next to Baltimore's Inner Harbor, this historical hike walks in the steps of our brave countrymen around the star-shaped Fort McHenry, where Francis Scott Key wrote the national anthem. In the early morning of September 13, 1814, British ships launched an attack on Fort McHenry during the War of 1812. The fort defended Baltimore's harbor from attacks. Key witnessed the twenty-five-hour bombardment and the strong defense during this Battle of Baltimore. When the British were forced to withdraw, a 30-by-42 foot American flag was hoisted. These events inspired Key to write "The Star-Spangled Banner."

For a fee, take a tour of the grounds. Stop by the visitor center to watch an orientation film, see exhibits, and visit the gift shop. Then take a self-guided tour of the fort. When you're ready to pound out some patriotic steps, hop on the gray brick sidewalk in front of the visitor and education center and next to the parking area. Facing the center, take the trail to the right and head toward the statue of Col. George Armistead. The statue and the fort and flag will be on your left. Armistead was the commander of the fort during the British bombardment. You'll be paralleling the entrance road for a few steps until you reach the official National Park Service sign. Take a left here to follow the path across the lawn toward the picnic area.

Ahead you won't be able to miss the larger-than-life statue of a man holding a harp. The bronze statue is not of Francis Scott Key, as many would assume. Rather, it represents Orpheus, the artful poet, musician, and singer of Greek mythology. The monument marks the centennial of the writing of the "The Star-Spangled Banner" and the defense of Baltimore. Standing 24 feet tall, the statue has a medallion honoring Francis Scott Key in its base. Take note of the trees lining the path, all dedicated to various colonels, majors, generals, and other heroes who played important roles in the battle.

Once you reach the picnic area, notice the redbrick building set to the right. This was once a Civil War magazine building used for safe storage of additional gunpowder and ammunition for the cannons. Built in 1864, the structure was converted into a rifle range during World War I. The fort served as an active military post into the 1900s.

After the picnic area you'll veer to the left to follow along the water and seawall. Choppy waves lap against the wall, the smell of salt lingers in the cool breeze from the water, and the sound of a CSX train whistle is common in the background. Be sure not to walk on the seawall! On your left, pass a memorial grove of Japanese cherry trees, originally planted in 1931, the same year "The Star-Spangled Banner" became the official national anthem. As you come to a bend in the trail, the Key Bridge stands straight ahead, as well as numerous freight and car-carrying ships, like the *Wallenius Wilhelmsen,* and sailboats and personal watercraft floating peacefully. More and more cannons come into sight by the fort, and a grandiose American flag stands tall and flies proudly.

Now, on the final leg of the loop, the 1st Mariner Bank Tower hovers over many city buildings, the Natty Boh beer sign is perched on a building just behind the tower, and a line of boat masts can be seen across the way. Just as you approach the back side of the visitor center, the taxi pier comes into view. Bear right to return to your starting point, and revel in the glory you will feel from this historical hike.

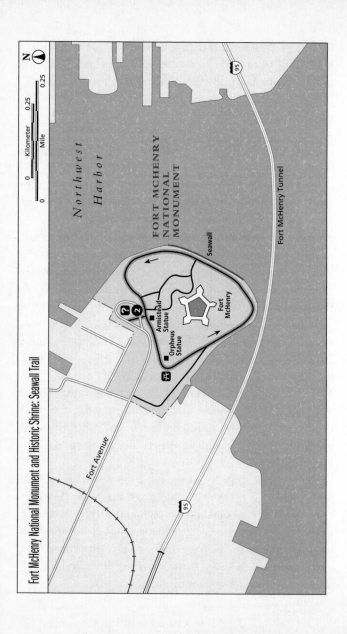

Fort McHenry National Monument and Historic Shrine: Seawall Trail

Miles and Directions

0.0   Facing the visitor center, take the gray brick path to the right, heading south toward the Armistead statue. You will reach the statue in just a few steps.

0.1   Reach the official National Park Service sign for Fort McHenry. Take a right to head toward the picnic area and giant statue of Orpheus.

0.2   Veer to the left to follow along the water and seawall.

0.3   Reach the memorial Japanese cherry grove.

0.6   You'll be directly across from the Canton industrial area.

0.8   Reach the back side of the visitor center and the side path to the water taxi pier.

3 Gwynns Falls Trail

While most of the 15-mile Gwynns Falls Trail is as urban as trails around Baltimore come, one section—from Leon Day Park to Windsor Mill Road—will surprise you with a thick tree canopy, river views, historical structures, and a variety of plant and animal species. The environment on the trail is a sharp contrast to the urban neighborhoods of west and southwest Baltimore City that the trail connects.

Distance: 3.6 miles out and back

Hiking time: About 2 hours

Difficulty: Moderate due to distance

Trail surface: Gravel, crushed stone

Best season: Year-round

Other trail users: Bicyclists, skaters, bird-watchers

Canine compatibility: Leashed dogs permitted

Fees and permits: None required

Schedule: Dawn to dusk; note that it is possible for trailhead parking areas with gates to sometimes stay locked until 8 or 9 a.m.

Maps: http://gwynnsfallstrail .org/images/pics/GFTMapFor Web.pdf

Trail contacts: 800 Wyman Park Dr., Ste. 010, Baltimore; (410) 448-5663; www.gwynnsfalls trail.org

Other: While this section is gravel, the rest of the trail is paved

Finding the trailhead: From I-695 take exit 16 for I-70 east/Local Traffic/Park & Ride. From I-70 take exit 94 for Security Boulevard. Stay in the right lane and turn right at the Ingleside Avenue traffic light. Cross the bridge and turn right at the top of the bridge (just before the Franklintown sign). Proceed 1 block to the stop sign at Franklintown Road and turn left. Proceed on Franklintown Road approximately 1.5 miles past the intersection with Winans Way, and the Winans Meadow Trailhead will be around the bend on the left. Continue for another 1.5 miles and reach the Leon Day Park Trailhead and parking lot on the right. GPS: N39 18.009'/W76 40.303'

The Hike

Hiding among row homes, concrete sidewalks, and traffic congestion, the 15-mile Gwynns Falls Trail brings some green to the otherwise gray surroundings. This linear greenway trail travels through west and southwest Baltimore City along the Gwynns Falls stream valley, a continuous trail connecting thirty neighborhoods. The section of trail from Leon Day Park to Windsor Mill Road, the only unpaved, gravel section, follows the route of an early-1800s millrace that carried water to power five mills. These mills turned Baltimore into one of the leading flour and textile producers in the nation. Along the hike learn about the history of the stream valley and the natural habitat through interpretive signs and historical heritage exhibits. You'll encounter hardwood species like white oak, American beech (uncommon in cities and urban areas), tulip poplar, sycamore, northern catalpa, and pin oak. You'll see locals fishing in the stream, out for a run or bike ride, or doing some bird-watching.

Begin the hike at Leon Day Park, named for Leon Day, a southwest Baltimore resident and ballplayer in the Negro Leagues who was inducted into the National Baseball Hall of Fame in 1995, six days before he died. Among other teams, he played for the Baltimore Black Sox in 1934 when African Americans were not allowed to play in the majors or minors. Today the park facilities include a baseball field, playground, and pavilion.

From the parking lot begin the hike by crossing a wooden bridge. You'll see green ovals painted on the ground with GF Trail in white writing. Follow the oval markers as you cross over Franklintown Road and then Morris Road. The path climbs uphill on Morris Road before it takes a turn back to

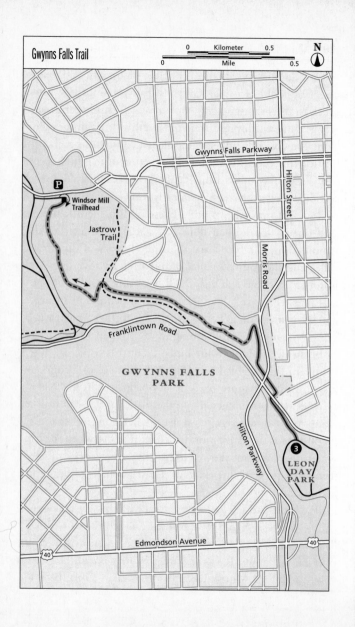

head into the woods. This is the point where the city fades into the background and the forest welcomes you on a wide, well-maintained, lush trail. The traffic noise is obvious in the beginning but soon becomes distant as the sound of the river grows stronger. Your hike from trailhead 4 (Leon Day Park) to trailhead 3 (Windsor Mills) will have benches for resting and a nice picnic table overlooking the river rapids below. Enjoy the city's green scene, truly a diamond in the rough!

Miles and Directions

0.0 Begin the trail at the Leon Day Park Trailhead.

0.1 Cross over Franklintown Road.

0.3 Cross over Morris Road. The trail heads uphill on Morris Road before entering the woods.

0.4 The trail doubles back sharply and heads into the woods.

0.9 Reach the first small trickle of a spring.

1.0 Reach a second spring.

1.3 Come to the intersection with the Jastrow Trail.

1.4 Reach an interpretive sign about Olmstead.

1.5 Cross a bridge surface.

1.7 Come to a picnic table with a view of the rapids below, soon followed by the Millstream interpretive sign.

1.8 Arrive at Windsor Mill Trailhead. Turn around and retrace your route back to Leon Day Park.

3.6 Arrive back at the parking lot and Leon Day Park Trailhead.

4 Cylburn Arboretum

Well-manicured lawns and lush landscaping with gardens and specimen trees are the backdrop for a total of 2.5 miles of trails on the arboretum grounds, combined with a museum and historic mansion.

Distance: 1.5-mile loop with spur
Hiking time: About 50 minutes
Difficulty: Easy
Trail surface: Natural, mulch, and turf
Best season: Year-round
Other trail users: Foot traffic only, bird-watchers
Canine compatibility: Leashed dogs permitted on the grounds and trails
Fees and permits: None required
Schedule: Park and buildings closed Mon. Spring and summer hours 8 a.m.–8 p.m., fall and winter hours 8 a.m.–5 p.m. The Vollmer Center is open 10 a.m.–4 p.m. daily.
Maps: Trail maps available at the visitor center, www.cylburnas sociation.org, or http://031dac8 .netsolhost.com/subpages/pdfs/ Cylburn%20Trails%20Map.pdf
Trail contacts: 4915 Greenspring Ave., Baltimore; (410) 367-2217; www.cylburnassociation.org

Finding the trailhead: From I-83 take the Northern Parkway west exit. Turn left on Greenspring Avenue. Continue past Cylburn Avenue and take the immediate left into the arboretum. Park in the visitor parking lot on the left side of the main entrance road. Follow the walking path toward the mansion house. GPS: N39 21.273'/W76 39.217'

The Hike

Minus the slight hum in the background of the Jones Falls Expressway, you'll soon forget that you are in Baltimore City and be taken over by the beauty and peacefulness of the arboretum. The lush grounds of the arboretum are manicured, with open lawns for picnicking or relaxing with a blanket and a book. You are surrounded by stunning display gardens, a nature museum, and the mansion house.

When you first arrive at the arboretum, you'll see the Vollmer Center, the visitor center, straight ahead as you drive up the main road. After parking, follow the paved path from the Vollmer Center toward the mansion. Turn left as you approach the mansion, and the trailhead is just behind the carriage house and nature center. When the leaves are off the trees, you may see highway on some sections of trail. But that doesn't stop seasonal birds like thrushes and warblers from chirping, woodpeckers from pecking, and deer from prancing about.

The arboretum was once the private estate of businessman Jesse Tyson. He was the president of Baltimore Chrome Works, a company that exported chromite throughout the world. The nineteenth-century Cylburn Mansion was originally built as a summer home for his mother and himself. Today you can enjoy the pristine grounds and the nature museum, open by appointment and on some weekends, housing a butterfly collection as well as displays of birds and eggs, fossils, rocks, and minerals. Explore the property to peek in the windows of the production greenhouses (not open to the public) and gardens scattered about. The hiking trails will take you through a variety of habitats.

At the trailhead signs are posted for the Circle Trail and the Woodland Trail. Start by walking north on the Woodland Trail, the old carriage road leading to the estate's private railroad stop. The trail heads slightly downhill until it ends just shy of the train tracks. Turn around and head back up the Woodland Trail to pick up the Ridge Trail, a short (⅛ mile) but steep hike uphill to the plateau. Join and follow the Azalea Trail to the left until the trail ends. Now make a sharp left turn and hop

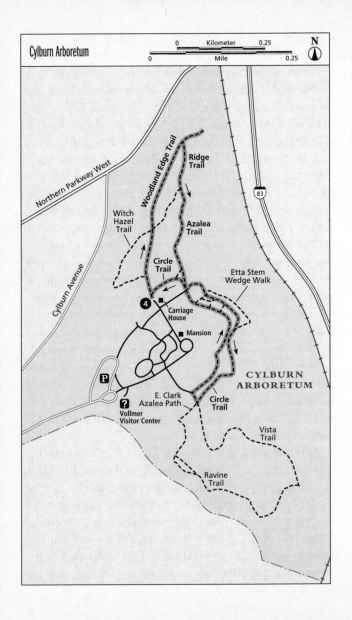

on the Circle Trail. Follow the Circle Trail until it meets the intersection of the Elizabeth Clark Azalea Path. Hang a right at this intersection (a fence and gate will be on your left) onto a partially graveled road and then another quick right through the narrow bamboo path to follow the Woodland Edge Trail or the "lawn border." You will cross a wooden bridge with a view of the mansion on the left and a line of tall trees. Hug the trail to the left. You will meet up again with the Circle Trail, the left fork of which takes you back to your starting point. Along the way you will have passed by gardens, spring wildflowers, viburnums, conifers, shrubs, and trees.

Miles and Directions

0.0 Find the trailhead just behind the carriage house and nature center. Your first landmark is the first intersection with the Witch Hazel Trail.

0.1 Come to the second intersection with the Witch Hazel Trail.

0.3 Pass the Ridge Trail intersection.

0.4 Trail ends at train tracks; turn around and take a left on the Ridge Trail.

0.5 Take a left on the Azalea Trail.

0.6 Continue left on the Azalea Trail.

0.7 Make a sharp left turn to get on the Circle Trail.

0.8 Cross the intersection with Etta Stem Wedge Walk.

1.0 Stay left on the Circle Trail.

1.1 Reach the intersection with the Elizabeth Clark Azalea Path; there is a cyclone fence gate on your left. Take the trail to the right.

1.3 Take a right on the Woodland Edge Trail through the bamboo forest.

1.4 Stay left on the Circle Trail at the fork.

1.5 Arrive back at the trailhead.

5 Gunpowder Falls: Jerusalem Village with Jericho Covered Bridge

Welcome to Jerusalem Mill Village, the home to Gunpowder Falls State Park headquarters. The mill here originally functioned as a grain mill from 1772 to 1961. The historic town buildings include a grist mill, blacksmith shop, gun shop, springhouse, and general store. This well-marked hike has much to offer, including historical sites, views of the Little Gunpowder River, and a covered bridge.

Distance: 3.2-mile figure-eight loop

Hiking time: About 1.5 hours

Difficulty: Moderate due to some uphill

Trail surface: Natural surface

Best season: Year-round

Other trail users: Mountain bikers, trail runners

Canine compatibility: Leashed dogs permitted

Fees and permits: None required

Schedule: Open 8 a.m. to sunset. Jerusalem Mill Museum and Visitor Center is open weekends 1–4 p.m.

Maps: Trail maps available at park headquarters

Trail contacts: 2813 Jerusalem Rd., Kingsville; (410) 592-2897; www.dnr.state.md.us/publiclands/central/gunpowder hereford.asp

Other: Summer concerts, war reenactments

Finding the trailhead: From I-95 take exit 74 to MD 152 west/ Mountain Road. Follow Mountain Road toward Fallston and turn left onto Jerusalem Road. Park in the lot on the right just before the mill. GPS: N39 27.750'/W76 23.447'

The Hike

A calm overwhelms you as soon as you enter the quaint and historic village of Jerusalem Mill, one of the oldest preserved mill villages in Maryland, located in Harford County. This area, rich in history, had a gun shop that supplied muskets during the early part of the Revolutionary War. Military reenactments sometimes take place here.

The calm continues as you head into the woods for a nature hike. You'll find the trailhead in the meadow behind and to the left of the Jerusalem Blacksmith Shop. Look for the white blaze on the tree just before you leave the grassy meadow and step on the natural trail surface. You'll be following the white-blazed trail for the first half of the loop and returning on the blue-blazed trail.

Where the trail crosses a small wooden bridge, a sign marks the site of an ice pond. It is presumed that it was once used to harvest ice in winter to be stored and used during the warmer months. At the first intersection with the blue-blazed trail, continue left to stay on the white trail, the Little Gunpowder Trail.

The next sign shares the history of the dam and start of the millrace. This dam once diverted water downstream via a race in order to power the grain mill and sawmill. The dam was abandoned in about 1940, and the grist mill was converted to electrical power until it went out of operation entirely.

After crossing a small stream followed by a slight uphill, the trail takes you away from the river to again intersect with the blue-blazed trail. This time you'll follow the blue trail to the right before passing power lines. The sound of the river rapids fades into the distance, but you'll hear the

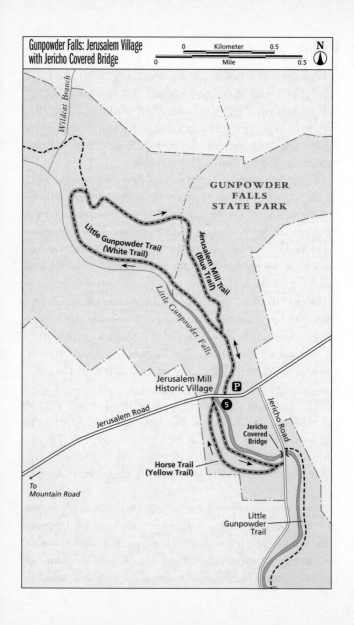

Gunpowder Falls: Jerusalem Village with Jericho Covered Bridge

Kilometer
0   0.5
Mile
0   0.5

N

Wildcat Branch

GUNPOWDER
FALLS
STATE PARK

Little Gunpowder Trail
(White Trail)

Jerusalem Mill Trail
(Blue Trail)

Little Gunpowder Falls

Jerusalem Mill
Historic Village

P

5

Jericho
Covered
Bridge

Jerusalem Road

Jericho Road

Horse Trail
(Yellow Trail)

To
Mountain Road

Little
Gunpowder
Trail

gurgle of a second small creek crossing. Follow the blue blazes on a sharp right turn downhill, heading back toward the river to follow a ridge above the river. Soon you'll meet back up with the white trail and pass by your original starting point.

Now continue on the white-blazed trail back to the center of town and cross over Jerusalem Road. Head to the right over the bridge. On the other side of the bridge, head down the stairs on the left and follow the trail along the water until you reach the intersection for the Horse Trail (yellow) and the trail toward the covered bridge. Of course, you have to check out the covered bridge. After you've had your fill, retrace your steps back to the intersection with the yellow trail. Follow the yellow trail all the way back to where you started. Enjoy the smell of honeysuckles and be sure to look for snakes!

Miles and Directions

0.0 Begin the trail in the meadow. Look for the white blaze on the tree. Follow the path and bear right to stay on the trail. After a few feet make a left turn to stay on the white-blazed trail.

0.1 Reach the historical marker for the millrace and waste gate.

0.2 Come to a historical marker at a wooden bridge for the ice pond, followed by the first intersection with the blue-blazed trail. Take a left at the fork and follow the white-blazed trail.

0.3 Reach the site of the old dam.

0.4 Come to a small stream crossing.

0.9 Follow the trail as it heads uphill. You will then reach the second intersection with the blue trail. Follow the blue trail to the right.

1.0 Pass by the power lines.

1.2 Continue to follow the blue trail to the right.

1.3 Come to a second creek crossing.

1.6 Reach an intersection where a trail continues straight and the blue-blazed trail takes a sharp turn to the right. Take the sharp right to stay on the blue trail.

1.7 Bear right to stay on the blue trail.

1.8 Meet back up with the white-blazed trail.

1.9 Return to the trailhead and continue straight toward Jerusalem Road.

2.0 Cross Jerusalem Road and head to the right to cross the bridge.

2.1 After crossing the bridge, go left down the stairs and then back onto the natural-surface trail. Keep left on the white-blazed trail for views of the water from the ridge.

2.3 Cross a small wooden bridge.

2.4 Reach the intersection with the Horse Trail (yellow). Stay left on the white trail to reach the covered bridge.

2.5 Reach the covered bridge and walk across. Retrace your route back to the intersection with the yellow trail.

2.6 Take the yellow Horse Trail to loop you back around.

3.0 Bear right to stay on the yellow trail.

3.1 Meet back up with the white-blazed trail to again cross the bridge back to the trailhead and parking lot.

3.2 Arrive back in Jerusalem Village and the parking lot.

6 Irvine Nature Center

This is a place where you will want to hike your own hike. Get some exercise and an education on a total of 6 miles of trails that wrap through meadows, forest, and wetlands and pass by various gardens, exhibits, and an overlook. The self-guided nature trails located on the grounds of this environmental education center are easy to follow. For instant gratification hike the short trail to the gazebo and overlook.

Distance: 0.4-mile loop
Hiking time: About 15 minutes
Difficulty: Easy
Trail surface: Natural packed dirt, grass, some paved
Best season: Year-round
Other trail users: Foot traffic only
Canine compatibility: No pets allowed
Fees and permits: Free entrance
Schedule: Nature center and trails open daily 9 a.m.–5 p.m.

Nature store open Mon to Fri 9 a.m.–5 p.m. and Sat and Sun 10 a.m.–4 p.m. Center closed on some holidays.
Maps: Trail maps available on website and in the nature center
Trail contacts: 11201 Garrison Forest Rd., Owings Mills; (443) 738-9200; www.explore nature.org
Other: Family and children's programs, school programs

Finding the trailhead: From I-695 west take exit 20 for MD 140 north toward Garrison. Turn right on Greenspring Valley Road and then left on Garrison Forest Road. The entrance is located across from the Jemicy School. GPS: N39 25.982' / W76 45.749'

The Hike

The Irvine Nature Center was founded in 1975 on the grounds of St. Timothy's School in Stevenson, its mission to educate and inspire the public to explore, respect, and protect nature. In 2000, 116 acres of land were donated by the state of Maryland to Irvine in the Caves Valley area. In 2008 the center relocated to its present location, surrounded by an additional 1,200 acres of land held in a conservation easement. Maryland has three major regions: mountains, piedmont (foothills), and coastal plain. The center and its grounds are representative of the piedmont region. The nature center guides you through the exploration of this type of region and what to expect of the land, habitat, and environment.

The building that houses the nature center is a "green" building displaying exhibits, many that are interactive, featuring artifacts, animal tracks, baby terrapins, a live demonstration beehive, and a kids' corner. In addition to the area's abundant wildlife, sixty-five resident animals call the center's grounds home. The center is a delightful place, home to attractions like the woodland garden full of Maryland native plants, an amphitheater, and a nature store. On your hiking adventure you can see an aviary, currently with residents such as a red-tailed hawk, screech owl, and barred owl. Pass by wildlife blinds, a camp shelter, and a Native American wigwam.

A quick hike on the Vista Loop Trail will take you to the gazebo overlooking the wide-open meadows and bordering tree line. It's the kind of view that conjures up feelings of freedom. The gazebo is a popular spot for couples tying the knot, so don't be alarmed if you happen to see some overly dressed hikers in suits and heels.

Just to the left of the nature center building, you can hop on the Vista Loop Trail and begin creating your very own adventure. Many of the trails have been dedicated in

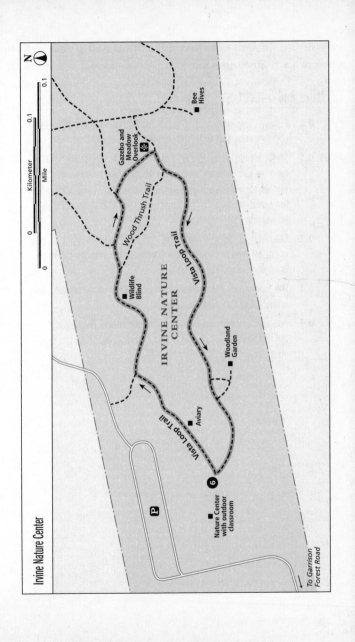

someone's honor. Signs describing this as well as educational signs are posted throughout the center grounds and trails.

Miles and Directions

0.0 Follow the path into the woods to the left of the nature center, following the trail signs for the Vista Loop Trail.

0.1 Make a right when the trail comes to a T. In a few steps be sure to check out the north wildlife blind. When the trail comes to a V, head left to stay on the Vista Loop. Come to the intersection with the Valley Wall Trail. Stay straight to remain on the Vista Loop.

0.2 Stay right to head toward the gazebo. Enjoy the view at the overlook meadow, and then continue the loop by following the Vista Loop Trail (south).

0.3 The trail veers left. In less than 0.1 mile, reach the gate and entrance to the woodland garden.

0.4 Pop back out at the outdoor classroom and picnic area just behind the nature center. Head uphill to return to the trailhead where you started.

7 Loch Raven Reservoir: Deadman's Cove

A quick and easy jaunt will lead you to the edge of the Loch Raven Reservoir, which supplies water for Baltimore City and most of Baltimore County. This trail is not heavily used and is often overgrown with tall grass. But it affords you a nice view and some solitude.

Distance: 1.2 miles out and back
Hiking time: About 30 minutes
Difficulty: Easy
Trail surface: Natural surface, grass
Best season: Year-round
Other trail users: Foot traffic only
Canine compatibility: Leashed dogs permitted
Fees and permits: None required
Schedule: Dawn to dusk

Maps: No trail maps available for the Loch Raven Reservoir Water Quality Management Area
Trail contacts: City of Baltimore Department of Public Works, Reservoir Natural Resources Section, 5685 Oakland Rd., Eldersburg; (410) 795-6151; www.baltimorecity.gov
Other: No facilities

Finding the trailhead: Take I-695 to exit 27 and drive north on Dulaney Valley Road. Cross Timonium Road. The trailhead is located a quarter mile past the entrance to Stella Maris Hospice. The parking lot for this trail accommodates about three cars, and the trailhead is on the opposite side of Dulaney Valley Road from the parking area. The parking area should not be confused with the larger lot a short distance down the road just past Old Bosley Road. GPS: N39 27.313'/W76 35.522'

The Hike

Is this a trail off the beaten path or on the beaten path? It's both, really. It's definitely a path less traveled, hence the solitude. But it is literally a beaten path as you follow a trail of beaten grass for a good portion. It's not terribly well maintained, but this trail to the water is a quick fix when you are looking for some peace and quiet with the reward of a nice view. Long pants are recommended due to high grass.

You'll recognize the trailhead by the orange line strung across the path. The hike starts out on a fire road, a wide grassy path that soon narrows, and the traffic noise from Dulaney Valley Road disappears after a few steps. You won't see any trail markers; rather, you'll be following the well-worn steps of the last person to tromp ahead of you. Expect to see some downed trees that you may have to climb over or skirt around. The path flip-flops between flattened grass and a natural packed dirt surface, and between spots that are shaded by pine forest and hardwoods and those that are very exposed.

At just about a half mile, you'll be walking on a spine of a few flat rocks. The largest of the flat rocks also marks the spot where you will see a well-worn trail to the right, heading toward the water. Follow this trail, which will lead you to the water's edge of the Loch Raven Reservoir. The reservoir is a popular spot for bass fishing, so why not pack your own fishing pole?

The reservoir provides drinking water for Baltimore City and most of Baltimore County. It occupies almost the entire central portion of Baltimore County. It's the largest of the three area reservoirs. The source of the reservoir water is Gunpowder Falls. While the destination is not necessarily ideal as a picnic spot, it is still a nice view of the water. Keep in mind that the main goal of the management of the reservoir area is water quality, and recreation trails are a secondary benefit. Therefore, the reservoirs and water quality

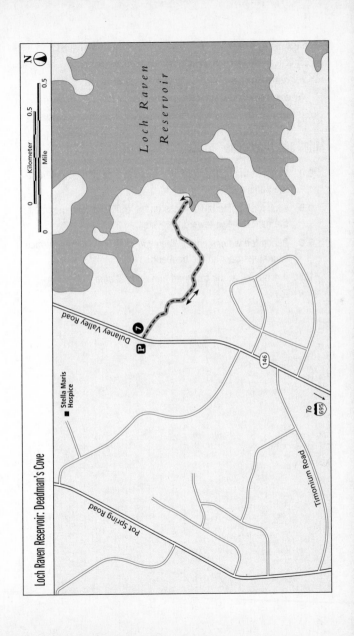

Loch Raven Reservoir: Deadman's Cove

management areas do not offer the same facilities and services you would find at a park or area specifically designed for recreation.

And while it's a spooky name for a hike's endpoint, the story behind the name Deadman's Cove remains a mystery.

Miles and Directions

0.0 Begin at the trailhead on the opposite side of the road from the parking lot.

0.5 Look for a spine of flat rocks on the trail, and take the trail to the right to head toward the water.

0.6 Reach the water's edge. When you have had your fill, retrace your steps back to the trailhead.

1.2 Arrive back at the trailhead and parking area.

8 Oregon Ridge: Loggers Loop

This hike is one of several trails at Oregon Ridge Nature Center. Follow a red-blazed path on natural surface through a forest of old logging trails, including a challenging ascent. It's a peaceful hike with a pond, a beach and swimming area, and a nature center topped off with a nice overlook of Hunt Valley.

Distance: 2.3-mile loop

Hiking time: About 1 hour

Difficulty: Moderate due to an uphill portion

Trail surface: Natural surface

Best season: Year-round

Other trail users: Hikers only

Canine compatibility: Leashed dogs permitted on trails

Fees and permits: None required

Schedule: Park grounds open daily from dawn to dusk; nature center open Tues through Sun 9 a.m.–5 p.m.; closed Mon

Maps: www.oregonridge.org/trails.php

Trail contacts: 13555 Beaver Dam Rd., Cockeysville; (410) 887-1815 for the nature center; (410) 887-1818 for the office; (410) 887-1817 for the beach; www.oregonridge.org

Other: Nature center with history, wildlife, and natural environment exhibits, and gift shop. Swimming allowed at Oregon Ridge Beach Memorial Day through Labor Day; fee for those ages 12 and up. Educational tours, programs, and festivals.

Finding the trailhead: If you're coming from I-83, take Shawan Road west and then make a left turn on Beaver Dam Road at the Oregon Grill. Just past the Oregon Grill, you will see a small red hut with signs in front of it directing you to the various areas of the park. Make a right following the arrow to the nature center. The trail begins at the bridge to the left of the nature center. GPS: N39 29.620' / W76 41.518'

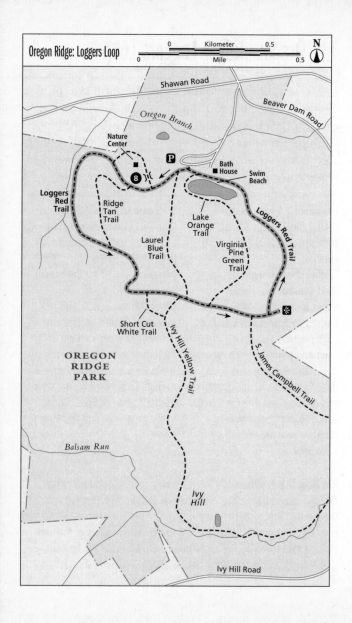

Oregon Ridge: Loggers Loop

0 Kilometer 0.5
0 Mile 0.5

N

Shawan Road

Oregon Branch

Beaver Dam Road

Nature Center

P

Bath House

Swim Beach

Loggers Red Trail

Ridge Tan Trail

Lake Orange Trail

Laurel Blue Trail

Virginia Pine Green Trail

Loggers Red Trail

Short Cut White Trail

Ivy Hill Yellow Trail

S. James Campbell Trail

OREGON RIDGE PARK

Balsam Run

Ivy Hill

Ivy Hill Road

The Hike

You'll feel like you are a world away when you step on the trails at Oregon Ridge Park. The land where the Oregon Ridge Nature Center now sits was an iron ore and marble mining operation during the mid-nineteenth century. The forest that once stood here during this time was clear-cut and sold for firewood. What you see now is a second-growth forest. The trails you see today were once logging roads used to drag out the trees after they were cut. The center was built in 1963 and houses displays on the history, wildlife, and environment of the park. It also has a library and gift shop. Oregon Ridge was also once a place for downhill skiing in the 1960s.

In total, the Cockeysville park has 1,043 acres in which to recreate. To the left of the nature center, begin your hike by heading over the bridge and following the well-marked red-blazed trail to the right. Along the way pass by streams, head up a solid incline, and enjoy a pleasant overlook of Hunt Valley. Many other well-marked trails intersect the Loggers loop trail in case you would like to get creative or add some distance to your hike. As the Loggers loop hike comes to an end, you'll pass by a beach, swimming area, and bathhouse before following the trail out the gate and back to the parking lot. Note that the gate is often locked in season. You may need to exit through the bath and concessions building.

Miles and Directions

0.0 Begin the trail to the left of the nature center. Cross over the bridge and head to the right to follow the Loggers loop trail marked with red blazes.

0.4 Start of the red trail.

0.7 Make a right at the T intersection.

0.8 Veer to the right to continue to follow the red blazes.

0.9 Reach an intersection with the white trail.

1.1 Reach the intersection with the yellow trail (Ivy Hill) on your right, immediately followed by the intersection with the blue trail (Laurel) on your left.

1.2 Reach the intersection with the green trail (Virginia Pine).

1.4 Bear left to continue to the top of the hill and the overlook.

1.5 On top of the hill, follow a small cutout trail clearing and unmarked trail to enjoy the views of the valley below. Then follow the trail on a gradual downhill.

1.8 The trail comes to a T at the bottom of the hill. Look to the left for a red blaze painted on a tree; it may be covered a bit with leaves and branches. Then make an immediate left on a wide path / gas line for a few steps. The trail takes another sharp right turn and goes back into the woods and down some stairs. Keep looking for the red blazes, as this short section can be a bit confusing.

1.9 See a frog pond on your right before passing through the picnic and playground area.

2.0 Arrive at the beach and waterfront area. Proceed in front of the concessions building and bathhouse.

2.1 Pass by a few more picnic tables before reaching the fence and gate. You'll exit through the gate; however, it is often locked in season. If so, exit through the bathhouse building. From here the red trail parallels the parking area before again entering the woods. Keep looking for red blazes.

2.2 End up back at the bridge you crossed at the trailhead and turn right.

2.3 Arrive back at the trailhead and parking area.

9 Prettyboy Reservoir: CCC Trail

Expect some solitude on this simple walk in the woods with sneak peeks of the Prettyboy Reservoir. The return trip includes a spur trail that ends at a scenic spot where you can take a load off and take in the waterfront view.

Distance: 3.8-mile lollipop loop with spur

Hiking time: About 1.5 hours

Difficulty: Moderate due to distance

Trail surface: Natural trail, packed dirt

Best season: Year-round

Other trail users: Foot traffic only

Canine compatibility: Leashed dogs permitted

Fees and permits: None required

Schedule: Dawn to dusk

Maps: No trail maps available for Prettyboy Reservoir Water Quality Management Area

Trail contacts: City of Baltimore Department of Public Works, Reservoir Natural Resources Section, 5685 Oakland Rd., Eldersburg; (410) 795-6151; www.baltimore city.gov

Other: No facilities

Finding the trailhead: From I-83 take exit 27 for Mount Carmel Road toward Hereford. Turn left on MD 137 west / Mount Carmel Road. Drive 3.9 miles and turn right onto Prettyboy Dam Road. After 1 mile turn left on the unmarked Traceys Store Road. Go 1.1 miles, where the road takes a sharp bend, and see the small parking lot on your right. Wooden posts with a strung cable mark the trailhead, along with a sign that reads Traceys Store Road Gate 4. The trailhead is easy to miss, so follow the directions closely. GPS: N39 37.195' / W76 44.116'

The Hike

If you are looking for solitude in a very rural setting, Prettyboy CCC trail should do the trick. It's located in the far northwest corner of Baltimore County and is not terribly well-known. The trail follows a wide fire road path until it loops. On the return you'll take a spur to a great spot overlooking the water, perfect for picnicking and fishing. Swimming, wading, and camping are not permitted, and boats are allowed by permit only. The trail out and the loop are not overwhelmingly scenic; the draw is the rather thick forest, the wildlife, and the peace and quiet. The highlight is on the spur trail on the return trip. If you choose, you can skip the loop portion altogether and head straight to the trail that meets the water's edge.

The Prettyboy Reservoir Watershed is the smallest and most remote of the three area reservoir watersheds. Deer, squirrels, turtles, and frogs call this area home, as well as a forest of pine, oak, and hickory trees.

The trail was cut by the CCC, or Civilian Conservation Corps, a public works relief program that operated from 1933 to 1942, providing jobs for young men who couldn't find work during the Great Depression. The labor jobs executed by the CCC were for the conservation and development of natural resources. And now they exist for your hiking pleasure!

Keep in mind that the main goal of the management of the reservoir area is water quality, and recreation trails are a secondary benefit. Therefore, the reservoirs or water quality management areas do not offer the same facilities and services you would find at a park or area specifically designed for recreation.

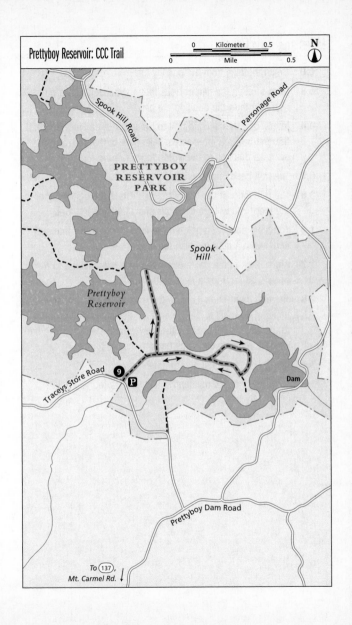

Kilometer

Mile

N

PRETTYBOY
RESERVOIR
PARK

Spook Hill Road

Parsonage Road

Spook
Hill

Prettyboy
Reservoir

Traceys Store Road

9

P

Dam

Prettyboy Dam Road

To 137,
Mt. Carmel Rd.

Miles and Directions

0.0 Begin the hike from the parking lot.

0.3 Pass through the first obvious trail intersection with a path narrower than the one you are on.

0.4 Intersect with a second trail to the left. The trail is wider than the first trail you intersected. Take note of the trail, as you will take this trail to the water on your return trip.

0.7 The trail heads uphill briefly.

0.8 The trail forks at the top of the hill. This is the beginning of the loop. You will return to this spot. Take the left fork.

1.4 You have almost completed the loop. Arrive at a T intersection. Make a right to finish the loop.

2.2 Arrive back at the trail intersection that will take you to the water's edge. Hang a right on this trail.

2.8 The trail dead-ends. Look to the left to see a very narrow trail heading downhill to the water. Take this steep trail downhill to the water's edge. Enjoy the views, and when you have had your fill, retrace your steps back to the main trail.

3.4 Reach the main trail and turn right.

3.8 Arrive back at the trailhead where you started your hike.

10 Robert E. Lee Park

An unexpected urban oasis borders the Baltimore City/Baltimore County line. This park beckons you to hike the little-known trails that follow the edge of Lake Roland and an abandoned railroad bed. Get a close-up look at Lake Roland Dam and enjoy the newly renovated park grounds.

Distance: 2.4-mile lollipop loop
Hiking time: About 1 hour
Difficulty: Easy
Trail surface: Natural surface, packed dirt, some paved
Best season: Year-round
Other trail users: Bicyclists, trail runners
Canine compatibility: Leashed dogs permitted (this is strictly enforced)
Fees and permits: None required
Schedule: Sunrise to sunset
Maps: Trail maps are currently a work in progress

Trail contacts: 1000 Lakeside Dr., Baltimore; (410) 887-4156; http://relpnc.org/; www.baltimorecountymd.gov/Agencies/recreation/programdivision/naturearea/relpark/index.htm
Other: The park is accessible by light rail train. These trains run often, and you will be crossing the tracks on this hike. Nature and educational programs, kayak tours, and campouts. There is an annual membership fee for the dog park, Paw Point.

Finding the trailhead: Take I-83 to the exit for Northern Parkway east. Turn left on Falls Road. Follow signs for the light rail and turn right into the light rail parking lot. Bear right to enter the park. The entrance road, Lakeside Drive, takes you past the dam to the left and dead-ends at the parking area. You'll walk the entrance road back to the dam to reach the dam bridge, where your hike will begin. Visitors may also park in the light rail parking lot and follow the boardwalk path to the dam. GPS: N39 22.673'/W76 38.650'

The Hike

After a major facelift, this 453-acre park once overrun by dogs and closed to the public for several years is now a local gem for hikers, trail runners, dog owners, and paddlers. After a renovation costing more than $6 million, the park, which is leased to Baltimore County, reopened in 2011. You'll find an outstanding network of trails, pavilions and grassy areas for picnicking, restroom facilities, a boat launch, and fishing platforms.

The area encompassing the park was part of a land grant from Lord Baltimore to several Maryland families. This park was originally constructed in 1861 as a reservoir and water source for Baltimore City and eventually for its surrounding counties. So why is the park named after Robert E. Lee? Well, it is said that an early benefactor to Baltimore City gave money for an equestrian statue to be erected in honor of Lee. Since there was already a statue of him in Wyman Park, the city did not initially spend the money. In 1944, the executor of the bequest thought that a nature park was a fitting memorial and authorized the use of the funds for the enhancement of the park.

The focal point is the Lake Roland Dam, where Lake Roland flows into the Jones Falls. After crossing the dam bridge, follow the paved path uphill for a grand view overlooking Lake Roland. When the paved path forks, veer left. When you reach a second pavilion, you'll see a natural trail and stairs on your left heading downhill. The trail takes you to the wooded area and trails surrounding Lake Roland. You'll have to cross the light rail tracks, so be cautious, as trains are frequent. The new rail bridge to your right is at the location of an earlier bridge that was destroyed by Southern sympathizers to prevent Northern troop movements early in the Civil War. Just after the tracks is the location where once stood the relay house station of the Baltimore & Susquehanna Railroad, which opened on July 4, 1831.

There is still much work in progress, including the trail system. At the time of publication, the trails have not yet been named and trail maps are currently unavailable. However, the trail described here is well worn and easy to follow even without trail markers.

Soon after stepping foot onto the natural surface, you'll see the remains of the old railroad bed. The wide dirt path is under tree cover, shaded, with a few muddy, narrow, and overgrown spots. The woodland and wetland environment is home to rare plant life and abundant wildlife. Deer roam freely, turtles plunk into the lake, eagles soar above, and frogs croak loudly. On the second half of the lollipop, the trail loops to the right until the water is on your left. When in doubt, hug the water and do not take any unmarked trails intersecting the path. When you again cross the tracks and return to the paved trail, hang a left to complete a paved loop. Pass the dog park on the left, Paw Point. This is not open to the general public; rather, an annual membership is required.

Miles and Directions

0.0 Your trail begins at the pedestrian bridge over the Jones Falls just below the dam. Cross the bridge to the paved pathway.

0.1 Pass the bathrooms on the left before following the paved path uphill. At the top of the hill, you'll see a pavilion on the right overlooking the dam.

0.2 The paved path forks. Take the trail on the left.

0.3 You will see a second pavilion on the right. Across from the pavilion is a natural trail and stairs that head downhill. Hang a left to hop on this trail.

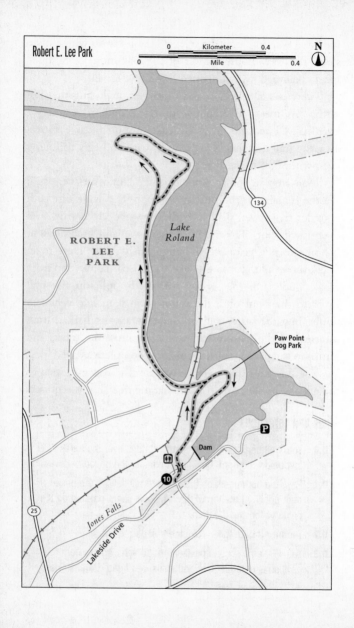

Robert E. Lee Park

ROBERT E. LEE PARK

Lake Roland

Paw Point Dog Park

134

25

Jones Falls

Lakeside Drive

Dam

10

N

Kilometer
0   0.4
Mile
0   0.4

0.4 Cross the rail tracks. Stay on the trail as it bears left.

0.8 A staircase on your right leads down to the water.

0.9 Take the trail to the left. This is the start of the loop. You will return to this spot.

1.1 Bear right halfway around the loop. At the intersection turn right to head back in the direction from which you came.

1.3 Continue straight on your trail. Do not take the side trail. Keep the water on your left.

1.4 Meet back up at the same spot where you began your loop.

2.0 Again meet up with the paved path across from the pavilion. Take a left on the paved path to close this second loop.

2.1 Reach the dog park on your left (membership required).

2.4 Arrive back at the hike's starting point.

11 Soldiers Delight: Serpentine Trail

For a hiking experience unlike any other in the area, hit the trails at Soldiers Delight National Environment Area (NEA) and take in this endangered ecosystem along the Serpentine Trail. Learn why it was named "serpentine" and enjoy the unique geological features and rare habitat.

Distance: 2.5-mile loop
Hiking time: About 1 hour
Difficulty: Moderate due to exposure
Trail surface: Packed dirt, gravel, crushed rock
Best season: Year-round
Other trail users: Hikers only
Canine compatibility: Leashed dogs allowed
Fees and permits: None required
Schedule: Sunrise to sunset. Visitor center open Sat and Sun 11 a.m.–3 p.m. and Mon through Fri by request; call ahead.

Maps: Trail maps available at park headquarters or at www.dnr .state.md.us/publiclands/ central/soldiersmap.asp
Trail contacts: 5100 Deer Park Rd., Owings Mills; (410) 922-3044; www.dnr.state.md.us/ publiclands/central/soldiers delight.asp
Other: The aviary is not open to the public, but there are enclosures that you may view if a staff member is available.

Finding the trailhead: Take I-795 to Franklin Boulevard west. Make a right on Church Road, a left on Berrymans Lane, and then a left on Deer Park Road. Use the parking lot on Deer Park Road, not the lot adjacent to the visitor center. GPS: N39 24.857' / W76 50.136'

The Hike

Don't get spooked by the snake reference! "Serpentine" actually refers to a type of rock formation likely named for its olive, gray, and green scaly appearance, which you will find on the trail.

In total, the Soldiers Delight NEA encompasses 1,987 acres and nearly 6 miles of hiking trails. It was named an NEA in 1968. The visitor center will give a peek into the history of the area and this sensitive ecosystem with its unique features. It's a protected area due to the serpentine soil, the nearly forty endangered plant species, as well as the insects, rocks, and minerals that can all be found here. The serpentine grassland and oak savanna ecosystem was part of the Great Maryland Barrens, an expansive area bare of timber. These barrens once covered more than 100,000 acres in Maryland, but today cover fewer than 1,000 acres. Serpentine rock is high in magnesium, originating 500 million years ago due to magma from under the ocean. It's dissolved by rainfall.

The restoration of this sensitive area is ongoing, and trail reroutes may be in place. Currently, prescribed burns are taking place to help rehabilitate the area and restore it to its natural serpentine habitat. Be sure to stay on the trail at all times. This NEA protects the largest undeveloped mass of serpentine bedrock in the eastern United States.

Soon after you start the trail from the very large parking lot, you'll pass by the visitor center, followed by an intersection with the Red Dog Lodge, once used as a hunting lodge and vacation getaway. The white-blazed path is well marked and easy to follow, but be warned that much of the trail is extremely open and exposed. Along the way the wide path flip-flops between forest, wetlands, and grassland habitats. Walk on jagged rocks, look for tadpoles in the creek crossing, and rock hop your way across a small stream. Be sure to look for the white wildflowers, serpentine chickweed, and read up on the ecosystem at the various educational signs.

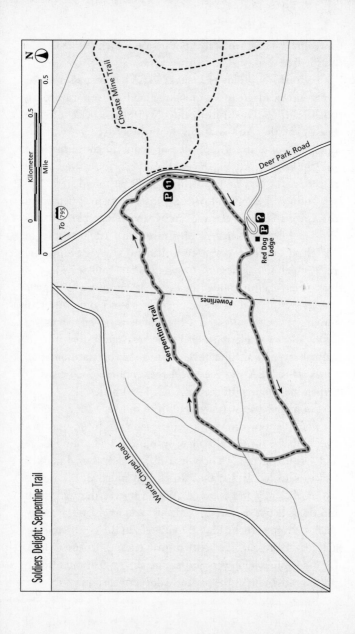

Soldiers Delight: Serpentine Trail

Not only is it a rare habitat, but Soldiers Delight was also the site of military encounters during the Civil War between Maryland Volunteers of the Confederate Army and the troops of the Union Army. An area rich in history, but not in soil! Enjoy hiking in this unique habitat located practically in your backyard.

Miles and Directions

0.0 Begin the trail by heading left toward the visitor center.

0.2 Reach a burned field.

0.3 Reach the visitor center and another parking area.

0.4 Reach the intersection with the trail to Red Dog Lodge. The trail continues to the right, but take a moment to visit the lodge, straight ahead.

0.5 Head under the power lines.

0.7 Come upon the second eco information sign.

1.0 See a barbed-wire fence on the left.

1.2 Take a quick hop across a small creek.

1.3 Rock hop across a second stream.

1.8 Pass another eco information sign.

1.9 Pass under power lines a second time.

2.3 Approach an information sign about serpentine rock.

2.5 Arrive back at the parking area.

12 Torrey C. Brown Rail Trail (NCR)

Formerly known as the Northern Central Railway Trail, this 20-mile, crushed-stone, abandoned railroad bed can be hiked in sections. Mostly covered by tree canopy, the well-maintained trail paralleling the Gunpowder Falls River is dotted with scenic overlooks, benches, and picnic tables.

Distance: 3.4 miles out and back

Hiking time: About 1.5 hours

Difficulty: Moderate due to distance

Trail surface: Crushed stone

Best season: Year-round

Other trail users: Runners, bicyclists, horseback riders

Canine compatibility: Leashed dogs permitted

Fees and permits: None required

Schedule: Trail closes at sunset

Maps: www.dnr.state.md.us/greenways/ncrt_trail.html

Trail contacts: 2813 Jerusalem Rd., Kingsville; (410) 592-2897; www.dnr.state.md.us/publiclands/central/tcb.asp

Other: Tubing, fishing; parking lots can get crowded.

Finding the trailhead: Take I-695 to I-83 north. Follow I-83 north to exit 27 for MD 137/Mount Carmel Road. Turn right (east) onto Mount Carmel Road. In 0.4 mile turn right at the traffic light onto MD 45/York Road. Make an immediate left at the next light onto MD 138/Monkton Road. Proceed 2.9 miles to the trail crossing and the parking lot on the left. The Monkton parking lot is one of the most popular on the trail. On weekends between Memorial Day and Labor Day, part of the lot is closed for the safety of bicyclists; street parking is limited and often fills early in the morning. GPS: N39 34.764'/W76 36.924'

The Hike

You will often hear this rail trail referred to as the NCR or the Northern Central Railway Trail, as it was named prior to the dedication to Torrey C. Brown. Dr. Brown, the third secretary of the Maryland Department of Natural Resources, had the vision for this multi-recreational trail, which was constructed in 1984.

The Northern Central Railway was built in 1832 and operated until 1872. It transported goods like flour, paper, milk, and coal from the small rural towns all the way up to York, linking them to Baltimore City. Abraham Lincoln rode this rail on his way to give the Gettysburg Address, and his body was delivered to Illinois via the NCR after his assassination.

The wide, flat, crushed-stone path draws all levels of outdoor enthusiasts from the neighbor out for a short stroll to the backpacker or the long-distance runner out to complete the entire 20-mile stretch. Under a canopy of trees, hike alongside the Gunpowder Falls River. On a hot day visitors splash in swimming holes and tubers float downstream. This trail has rewards around every corner, from bridges and scenic overlooks to ruins and rapids. The trail starts in Cockeysville, Maryland, and ends just over the Pennsylvania line in New Freedom.

A recommended easy, flat section begins in Monkton, the site of the restored Monkton Station, a historic train station that now houses a museum, gift shop, and ranger station. From there you will head north until you reach some old railroad remains. Head back the way you came, or if you are feeling ambitious, continue your trek north or south to discover what is around the next bend. In addition to mile

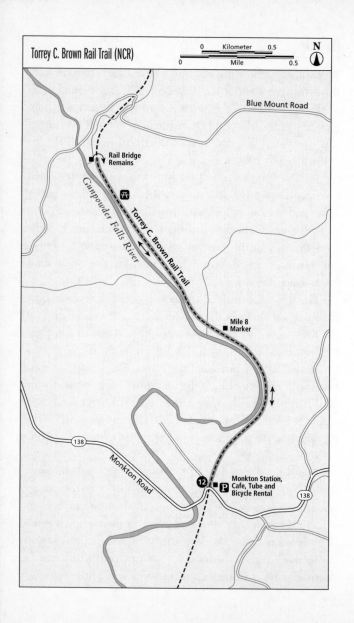

markers along the way, you'll see white "W" markers. These do not indicate water, as some might assume. Rather, they are a look back in time, as these are train whistle signals. These signs informed railroad engineers to begin sounding their whistle at that location.

At the end of your long hike, reward yourself with a sandwich and ice cream from the take-out restaurant and cafe located at the parking area. There is a parking lot and street parking at Monkton, as well as restrooms, water, and picnic tables. This place is a paradise for outdoor enthusiasts, and in peak weather don't be surprised to see crowds of people at the parking area unloading bikes, strapping on water belts, lacing up their hiking shoes, and rolling inner tubes down the road to get in on a piece of outdoor action. The Torrey C. Brown Trail is part of the larger Grand History Trail route, which connects the historic cities of Annapolis, Baltimore, Frederick, Gettysburg, Washington, and York.

Miles and Directions

0.0 Start at the Monkton Station parking lot.

0.4 Come to a bench.

0.5 Reach an educational sign about ferns.

0.8 You will see a sign for mile marker 8 followed by a bridge crossing.

1.1 Reach yet another bench followed by some picnic tables.

1.7 Reach a final bench and railroad ruins at the turnaround point. Turn around and retrace your route back to parking area.

3.4 Arrive back at Monkton Station.

13 Rocks State Park: Falling Branch

A quick out-and-back hike in the Falling Branch area of Rocks State Park couldn't be more rewarding when the destination is Maryland's second-highest vertical waterfall, Kilgore Falls.

Distance: 1.1 miles out and back with spur

Hiking time: About 30 minutes

Difficulty: Easy

Trail surface: Dirt path and short bridge and boardwalk

Best season: Year-round

Other trail users: Runners, horseback riders

Canine compatibility: Leashed dogs permitted

Fees and permits: None required

Schedule: Open 9 a.m. to sunset Apr through Oct and 10 a.m. to sunset Nov through Mar

Maps: http://www.dnr.state .md.us/publiclands/central/ rocksmap.asp

Trail contacts: Rocks State Park, 3318 Rocks Chrome Hill Rd., Jarrettsville; (410) 557-7994; www.dnr.state.md.us/ publiclands/central/rocks

Other: Trail offers a nice swimming hole but there is no lifeguard on duty. There are no facilities such as restrooms or picnic tables.

Finding the trailhead: From US 1 north / Belair Road toward Bel Air, exit on MD 24 north / Rock Spring Road toward Forest Hill and Rocks. At the roundabout stay straight on MD 24 / Rocks Road. Turn left on St. Mary's Road, and then turn right on Falling Branch Road. The parking lot will be on your right. The lot fills up fast on weekends and holidays. No parking is allowed on Falling Branch Road. GPS: N39 41.402' / W76 25.391'

The Hike

The Falling Branch area of Rocks State Park is a 67-acre parcel of land located 5 miles north of the main body of the 855-acre park. The biggest reward on this wooded hike is the second-highest natural vertical waterfall in Maryland, Kilgore Falls. Though it was once a meeting place for Susquehannock Indians, in recent years few people knew about this gem. The waterfall was located on private property until it was donated to the state of Maryland and opened to the public in 1993. This area of northern Harford County used to bustle with mills, farms, tanneries, and stills dating back to the 1700s. However, it was mostly abandoned in the 1900s once the railroad shut down and farmers didn't have a way to get their crops to Baltimore markets.

The wooded path will take you over a footbridge and boardwalk as you make your way to the falls, following Falling Branch stream, a tributary of Deer Creek. Falling Branch stream passes through a steep gorge known as Kilgore Rocks. Along the way you'll see a few hemlock trees, oaks, and lots of maples. Look for white-tailed deer, red fox, wild turkey, black snakes, black racers, and a variety of birds like woodcocks. If you are really lucky, you might even see an eagle. This environmentally sensitive area is also host to a family of beavers, but be sure to enjoy the wildlife from a distance.

About halfway down the footpath, 150 feet past the bench, look to the left for the remains of what is said to be an old farmstead comprising a two-story wood-frame home with a massive chimney. The trail comes to a Y, and you can choose to go to the right, to the top of the falls, or left, where you will come to a water crossing, Falling Branch stream, with nicely placed rocks and stepping stones. After crossing

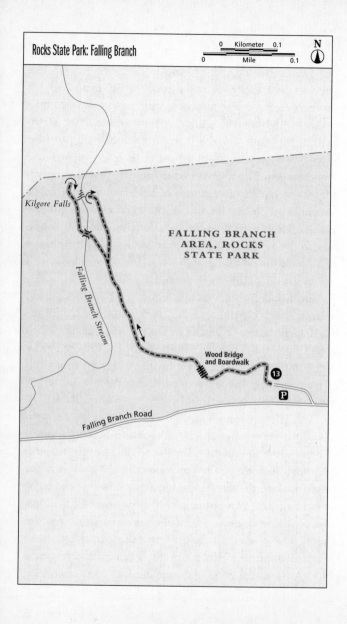

0   Kilometer   0.1

0   Mile   0.1

N

Kilgore Falls

FALLING BRANCH
AREA, ROCKS
STATE PARK

Falling Branch Stream

Wood Bridge
and Boardwalk

13

P

Falling Branch Road

the stream, the trail continues right to the base of the impressive falls, surrounded by huge boulders and rock formations. According to the Maryland Geological Survey, the waterfall is 17 feet tall but the rocks that form the gorge around the falls are about 34 feet. Take a dip and reenact the waterfall scene, filmed at Kilgore Falls, from *Tuck Everlasting,* starring Alexis Bledel and Jonathan Jackson. Note that the rocks are slippery and there is no lifeguard on duty.

Miles and Directions

0.0 Start at the trailhead adjacent to the parking lot.

0.2 Reach a bench.

0.3 Look down to the left to see the remains of an old stone foundation of a mill and farmhouse. When you reach the Y intersection, take the right-hand trail to go to the top of the falls.

0.4 Arrive at the top of the falls and return the same way back to the Y intersection.

0.5 From the intersection take the trail down to the river and water crossing. Once across, follow the trail to the right.

0.6 Cross a short wooden footbridge and arrive at Kilgore Falls. Trace your steps back to return to the trailhead and parking area.

0.7 Arrive back at the Y intersection.

1.1 Arrive back at the trailhead.

14 Piney Run Park: Lake Trail Loop

Hug the water's edge of a 300-acre lake on one of several hikes on a total of 5 miles of trails. Plan to spend the day at the park enjoying facilities like boat rentals, fishing, picnicking, playgrounds, tennis courts, and a nature center.

Distance: 1.1-mile loop
Hiking time: About 30 minutes
Difficulty: Easy
Trail surface: Natural, packed dirt, short road walk
Best season: Spring, summer, fall
Other trail users: Mountain bikes allowed on specified trails
Canine compatibility: Leashed dogs permitted
Fees and permits: Fees are charged, less for Carroll County residents

Schedule: Open 7 a.m. to sunset daily from Apr 1 through Oct 31
Maps: Trail maps available at park entrance or at http://cc government.carr.org/ccg/recpark/ pineyrun/docs/trail-guide.pdf
Trail contacts: 30 Martz Rd., Sykesville; (410) 795-5165; www.pineyrunpark.org
Other: No wading or swimming allowed

Finding the trailhead: Take I-695 to exit 18. Merge onto MD 26 west/Liberty Road toward Randallstown. Drive 14.2 miles and turn left on White Rock Road. Go 1.3 miles and turn left on Martz Road. Follow signs to the boat ramp for parking. The hike begins next to the pier at the far right of the boathouse. GPS: N39 23.865'/W76 59.109'

The Hike

Make a day out of your visit to Piney Run Park. Your pre- or post-hiking activities could include kayaking, canoeing, playing on the playground, tennis, or exploration at the nature center and gift shop. The nature center features live animals like snakes, turtles, fish, tarantulas, and toads. Check out the exhibits and interactive displays or join a program led by a park naturalist. There are also raptor cages in the back with various birds of prey. Pick up a trail map at the entrance gatehouse and combine a couple of trails to build your own hike, or enjoy the short Lake Trail loop as described here.

The US Army Corps of Engineers built the 300-acre lake in 1974. Piney Run is a hot spot for fishing. Along the trail you'll see several fishing platforms and floating piers. Pack a picnic and take in the view from one of the platforms. Or bring your rod and try your hand at catching a largemouth bass, yellow perch, or catfish, all common in the lake. The trail is narrow and overgrown in some spots. The Lake Trail begins near the pier to the far right of the boathouse and hugs the water. At one point you'll see a boardwalk down along the water and a natural trail on a higher path. Take either, as they eventually merge back into one trail.

As you continue, the nature center will come into view on your right through the trees. A small unmarked trail will take you to the center. Or continue to follow the water to the Yak Shack, a storage shed for kayaks. Shortly after the Shack, the trail fades a bit and a trail to the right becomes obvious. Take this trail, which will lead you to the Inlet Trail.

The Inlet Trail is likely the most popular in the Piney Run Park trail system, with a length of 3.1 miles. Here the Inlet Trail heads left and right. Hang a right to continue the loop back in the same direction from which you came. The Inlet Trail dead-ends at the park road. A quick left and then right will put you back on the entrance road you drove in on. Follow it back to the trailhead. Then rent a canoe or kayak at the boathouse to cool off with a paddle on the lake!

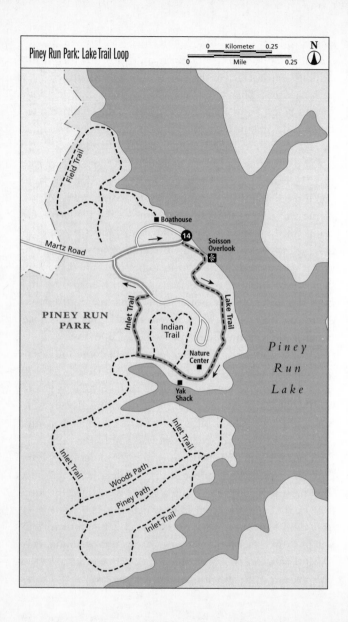

Piney Run Park: Lake Trail Loop

N

0   Kilometer   0.25
0   Mile   0.25

Field Trail

Boathouse

Martz Road

14

Soisson Overlook

PINEY RUN PARK

Inlet Trail

Indian Trail

Lake Trail

Nature Center

Piney Run Lake

Yak Shack

Inlet Trail

Inlet Trail

Woods Path

Piney Path

Inlet Trail

Miles and Directions

0.0 Begin at the trailhead with a sign marked Lake Trail. Walk up two sets of stairs and past a boardwalk platform with picnic tables on your left with a nice view of the lake Soisson Overlook. This will be followed by a second platform and boardwalk.

0.1 A boardwalk on the left will walk you along the water, or take the natural path on the high road. They both merge back into one trail.

0.5 You'll see the nature center through the woods on your right and an unmarked trail leading to it.

0.6 Reach the Yak Shack.

0.7 The trail around the water fades and you'll come to an unmarked trail on your right. Follow the unmarked trail uphill to the intersection with the Inlet Trail. When you reach the intersection, take a right to head back in the direction from which you came.

0.9 The trail dead-ends at the park road. When you reach the road, bear left. You'll intersect with the main entrance road you drove in on. Hang a right to head back down to the parking area, lake, and trailhead.

1.1 Arrive back where you started.

15 Centennial Park Lake Loop

A loop hike around a man-made lake in Centennial Park, Howard County, takes you over bridges, past ball fields and pavilions, and through woodlands, wetlands, and an arboretum. Home to a wide variety of wildlife, the lake is used for the conservation of various fish types.

Distance: 2.5-mile loop
Hiking time: 1.25 hour
Difficulty: Easy
Trail surface: Paved surface
Best season: Year-round
Other trail users: Bicyclists, runners
Canine compatibility: Leashed dogs permitted in the park but not in picnic, playground, or sporting areas
Fees and permits: No fee required; pavilions and sports fields are available by permit
Schedule: Open 7 a.m. to dusk

Maps: http://www.centennialmd .org/index.php?dove=maps
Trail contacts: 10000 MD 108, Columbia; (410) 313-7271 or (410) 313-7256; www.centennial md.org
Other: Swimming is not allowed in the lake. Canoe, kayak, paddleboat, and rowboat rentals available Mon through Fri 11 a.m.–6 p.m. and Sat and Sun 9 a.m.–6 p.m. mid-Apr through mid-Sep.

Finding the trailhead: From I-70 take US 29. From US 29 take MD 108 west toward Clarksville. The main entrance to the park is about 1 mile ahead on your right. Trailhead is located at the boat ramp and parking area. GPS: N39 14.501'/W76 51.523'

The Hike

Centennial Park is a jovial place with paddlers cruising the water, kids playing on the playground, picnickers enjoying an afternoon, and of course those out for an easy but scenic hike around beautiful Centennial Lake. The park itself, with 325 acres, has lots of amenities including fishing, boat rentals, a boat launch area, ball fields, picnic areas, tennis and volleyball courts, a skate area, playgrounds, and concession stands.

But a stroll around the entire lake offers the best opportunity for scenery and serenity, as you may see an abundance of wildlife and wildflowers. Common to the area are great blue herons, swallows, bluebirds, turkey vultures, green herons, mallard ducks, Canada geese, bald eagles, and hawks. Also look for rabbits, red fox, beavers, snakes, and turtles, as well as monarch and swallowtail butterflies frolicking in this pleasant environment. And of course, ducks love Centennial Lake.

The park is a popular spot for running races, walk-a-thons, and triathlons. The trails sees a good amount of traffic, including bicyclists, skaters, dogs trotting along with their owners, and parents pushing strollers. There is plenty of parking to accommodate the many visitors to the park.

The trail takes you past many park facilities, over bridges, and through the Centennial Arboretum, which has no fences or boundaries but is rather just an uninterrupted part of the natural experience, with interpretive signs and identification tags labeling the diverse species of flora and trees like hickory, oak, walnut, dogwood, and beech.

You'll begin your hike at the boat ramp and pavilion area. The trail here is exposed. But soon, heading toward the opposite side of the lake, you will enter a canopy of trees and pass through the arboretum. As you cross over the scenic steel bridge, look for paddlers below, as well as the largemouth bass, rainbow trout, and catfish that have made their home here in Centennial Lake. Part of the trail exposes its travelers to picturesque marshes and wetlands with cattails and lily

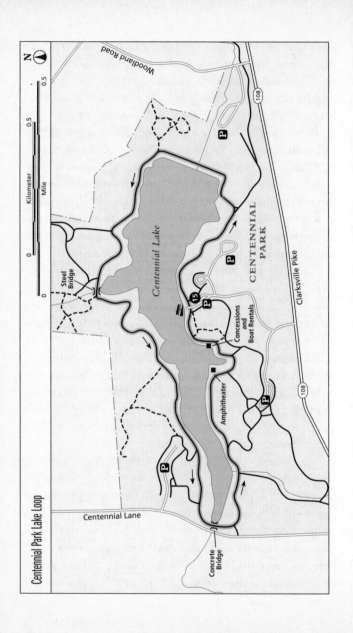

Centennial Park Lake Loop

pads. As you pass by several ball courts, remember that hiking is just one of the recreational activities on the lake. Hug the water and remain on the path ahead, as several paved offshoots will take you to various parking areas.

As you get closer to closing the loop, you'll pass by the amphitheater, which hosts a variety of cultural performances, and then restrooms, concession stands, and boat rentals. Swimming is not permitted in the lake. I don't know about you, but an ice cream and a paddleboat ride would certainly make this a memorable outing!

Miles and Directions

0.0 Begin your hike at the boat ramp. Head to the right to follow the paved trail.

0.1 See the pavilions on the right.

0.4 See a playground just off the trail.

0.7 Reach the arboretum.

1.0 Cross a steel bridge.

1.6 Come to the ball courts.

1.7 Cross a concrete bridge.

2.2 Hike past the amphitheater.

2.3 Reach the concessions and boat rental area.

2.5 Arrive back at where you started.

16 Patapsco Valley State Park: Grist Mill Trail—Lost Lake to Ilchester Road

This is an easy yet scenic hike along a paved rail trail, passing two swinging bridges, an old viaduct, and a dam. Following the path of the original roadbed of the Baltimore & Ohio Railroad, the trail parallels the river on the left and the railroad bed on the right, passing several historic sites.

Distance: 5.0 miles out and back
Hiking time: About 2.5 hours
Difficulty: More strenuous due to distance
Trail surface: Paved
Best season: Year-round
Other trail users: Bicyclists, runners, horseback riders, skaters
Canine compatibility: Leashed dogs permitted
Fees and permits: Fees charged are less for residents and on weekdays.

Schedule: 7 a.m. to sunset
Maps: Trail maps available for purchase at ranger station or at www.dnr.state.md.us
Trail contacts: 8020 Baltimore National Pike, Ellicott City; (410) 461-5005; www.dnr.state.md .us/publiclands/central/ patapsco.asp
Other: Fishing, cross-country skiing

Finding the trailhead: Take US 1 south toward Arbutus. Turn right on South Street. The park entrance is on the left. Once you enter through the gate, you'll see the ranger station, beyond which is an intersection. You will turn right and then follow the bend in the road to the left, following the sign that reads upper and lower Glen Artney Road. At the end of the road are two parking lots and a lake. The trailhead marker is next to the restroom. GPS: N39 13.814' / W76 43.699'

The Hike

So, what is a grist mill anyhow? Well, it's a place where grain is ground into flour, meaning this trail is aptly named in part for the Orange Grove Flour Mill, which was once in operation on this site. It burned in 1905, but ruins can still be seen on the opposite side of the first swinging bridge. In general, the Patapsco area was a prime site for America's Industrial Revolution due to waterpower and the railroad. Bloede Dam, located near the end of the trail before Ilchester Road, made it possible to power iron, paper, grist, and textile mills. It was the world's first submerged hydroelectric plant. The famous swinging bridge that you see along the trail was used by flour mill workers walking from their company-owned community across the river to the factory on the east side of the river. And remnants of the railroad can be seen along the path.

The trail starts at Lost Lake, which has an overlook platform great for fishing. Just past the lake a trail kiosk marks the official start of the trail. There is a restroom at the edge of the parking lot. The paved trail, which follows the river to your left and the train tracks on your right, uses the original B&O Railroad right-of-way. Today the tracks just above the trail are in use by CSX, so expect to see a train or two pass by. The original B&O crossed the Patapsco River atop the Patterson Viaduct. You'll pass by one single stone arch, the remains of the viaduct's stone abutments, and a multiple-stone-arch railroad bridge, among other signs of early development like stone walls and culverts.

This is a popular trail for mountain bikers, runners, and moms with strollers. The trail is shaded as it passes through a forest of trees and several river rapids. Many enjoy fishing,

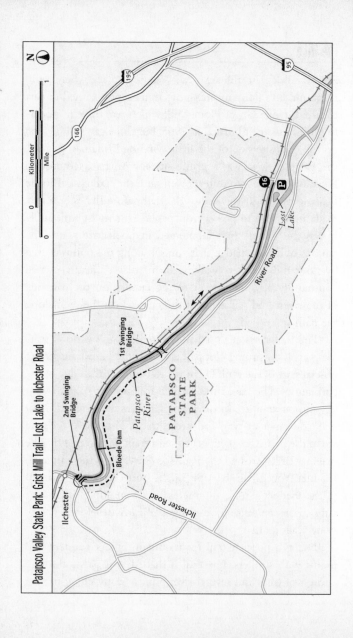

Patapsco Valley State Park: Grist Mill Trail—Lost Lake to Ilchester Road

swimming, and wading in the water. Picnic benches and waterfront areas make great spots for picnicking. The last mile of the trail is an extension of the original trail, including a second suspension bridge for hikers and bicyclists only, with outstanding views of the Patapsco River. Patapsco Valley is one of Maryland's oldest state parks, with roughly 16,000 acres for recreation.

Miles and Directions

0.0 Head toward Lost Lake next to the parking area and the trail kiosk at the edge of the lot. The trail begins upriver.

0.4 Reach the intersection with the Vineyard Spring Trail.

0.8 Cross over a wooden bridge.

1.3 On the right see the mill ruins.

1.5 On your left you'll see the swinging bridge. You will continue to stay straight on the Grist Mill Trail.

1.8 Cross a cement bridge and see the Patterson Viaduct remains on your right.

2.4 Bloede Dam can be seen on the left with a slightly obstructed view.

2.5 Come to the second swinging bridge, marking the end of the trail. Turn around and retrace your route back to the car.

5.0 Arrive back at Lost Lake and the parking area.

17 Downs Memorial Park

Start and end this loop trail with expansive views of the Chesapeake Bay and Bodkin Creek inlet. A perimeter trail takes you on a paved, curvy path along a wooded corridor through forest and marshland.

Distance: 3.7-mile loop
Hiking time: About 1.75 hours
Difficulty: Moderate due to distance
Trail surface: Paved; natural-surface extension trail options
Best season: Year-round
Other trail users: Runners, bicyclists, skaters
Canine compatibility: Leashed dogs permitted
Fees and permits: Vehicle fee; season pass available for all four paid-entry Anne Arundel County parks
Schedule: 7 a.m. to dusk; it's best to call ahead for the specific closing time. Closed Tues. Visitor center hours are Mon, Wed, Thurs, and Fri 9 a.m.–4 p.m. and Sat and Sun 10 a.m.–4 p.m. Closed Thanksgiving and Christmas Day.
Maps: Trail maps available at entrance gatehouse, visitor center, and www.aacounty.org/RecParks/parks/downs/map.cfm
Trail contacts: 8311 John Downs Loop, Pasadena; (410) 222-6230, events line (410) 222-6239; www.aacounty.org/RecParks/downs
Other: No swimming allowed, dog beach open to the public, kayak/canoe launch, concerts at the amphitheater

Finding the trailhead: Take I-695 to I-97 south. Then take exit 14 to MD 100 east. Take a slight right on Mountain Road east. Drive 3.7 miles and continue on Pinehurst Road. Follow signs to the park, and take a right into the entrance at Chesapeake Bay Drive. GPS: N39 06.607'/W76 26.015'

The Hike

Ah, that bay breeze is so alluring. It's a great way to start and end your hike on the Perimeter Trail in Downs Memorial Park. With 236 acres, the park has many facilities including bathrooms, water fountains, dog beach, fishing pier, playground, and picnic area. There are a total of 5 miles of paved hiking trails and a network of natural-surface interior trails.

The trailhead for the Perimeter Trail is just behind the visitor center and off to the right. You'll see the bridge to the James A. Moore Memorial Overlook. Before you cross the bridge, a staircase on your right takes you down to the paved trail. When you reach the bottom of the stairs, take a right on the paved path to begin your loop. One of the first sights you'll see is a fitness station, one of several, that could use a little TLC. The trail is well marked with short wooden mile-marker posts placed every tenth of a mile as well as directional markers. You'll find plenty of shade as you curve your way through mature forest and marshy areas.

In the early morning you may see red and gray foxes and raccoons. It's not uncommon to see deer, pileated woodpeckers, turkey vultures, ospreys, and black, white, and red squirrels. If you hear some sort of critter scurrying among the leaves, it's a good chance you've found a skink. These lizards scurry about. Look for the juvenile lizards with blue tails and the plump adults with red-and-brown heads. The park is home to three species of native orchids; ferns; red maple trees; mountain laurel; dogwoods; black walnut trees; white, black, and chestnut oak trees; and wildflowers like wood aster and spotted jewelweed.

Surprisingly, there is a good amount of solitude to be found on this trail. Although the buzz of traffic remains in the background, the scenery will set your mind free. Several benches are placed along the trail to help you take it all in. At just over a mile, you'll see the gatehouse where you first entered the park. Along the path a short side trail and two boardwalks will take you to the water's edge to get a close-up view. Look for turtles, minnows, perch, skates, and water snakes. You'll also pass the dog beach and Downs Park Fishing Pier, a 330-foot pier extending into the Chesapeake Bay. Toward the end of the hike, the trail opens up for stunning views of the bay, and the Bay Bridge can be seen in the distance. As you head back to the parking area, take a moment to walk through Mother's Garden on your left, a Victorian-style garden known as the "wedding nook."

The Bodkin Neck peninsula was once farmland known as Deer Park Farm, producing veggies and fruits to be shipped to the Baltimore markets by sailboat. In the early 1900s the wealthy Baltimorean H. R. Mayo Thom family made the farm their summer estate and renamed it Rocky Beach Farm. The Bishop Family from Baltimore was the next to own the farm, until it was purchased by Anne Arundel County in the mid-1970s and opened to the public in July 1982 as Downs Memorial Park. The park is named for John (Jack) Downs, a public servant of the county, as a tribute to his dedicated service to the residents. Downs served as county councilman in this district.

Miles and Directions

- **0.0** Begin the trail at the stairs headed downhill, just before the bridge to the overlook.
- **0.1** Reach the first of many fitness stations and the 0.1-mile-marker post.

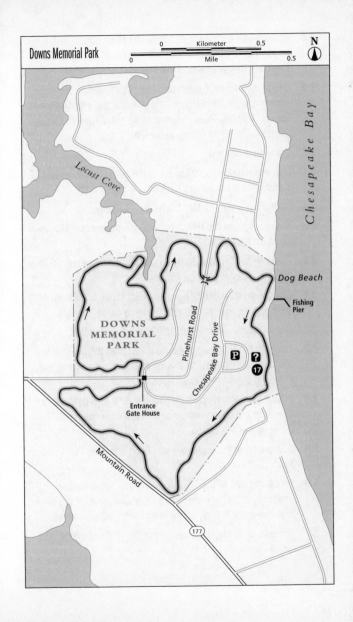

Downs Memorial Park

Kilometer
0   0.5
Mile
0   0.5

N

Chesapeake Bay

Locust Cove

Dog Beach

Fishing
Pier

DOWNS
MEMORIAL
PARK

Pinehurst Road

Chesapeake Bay Drive

P

?

17

Entrance
Gate House

Mountain Road

177

0.5 A boardwalk on the left heads to Mountain Road. Continue on the paved perimeter trail, which soon intersects with the Eco Trail. This intersection is unmarked.

1.3 Reach the entrance gatehouse. Do not cross over the entrance road. Rather, turn right to follow the crosswalk across Pinehurst Road. After crossing, you'll want to follow the paved trail that heads to the left.

1.5 Come to a pavilion.

2.1 Follow the trail for a few steps to the left to the water and bench until it places you back on the paved path.

2.4 Take a left when the trail comes to a T intersection.

2.6 Stay straight on the paved path at the intersection with an unmarked paved trail.

2.8 Continue to stay straight when you come to a bench on your left and a paved path on your right.

2.9 Cross a wooden bridge over Pinehurst Road, soon followed by a parking area on the left. Continue to stay straight.

3.0 See a boardwalk for Pinehurst Crossing on your left.

3.2 Come to the Brightwater Pavilion. Just past the pavilion follow the perimeter trail to the left toward the restrooms and following signs to the dog beach.

3.3 Follow a boardwalk path on your left for a look at the water. Return to the paved path, and in a few more steps you'll arrive at the dog beach.

3.4 See the fishing pier on your left. Soon after, the Fernwood Pavilion will be on your right.

3.5 Follow the trail to the left just before you reach the playground. The trail opens up with expansive views of the water, and the visitor center, where you started, comes into view.

3.7 Arrive back at the steps heading uphill to the overlook and visitor center.

18 Kinder Farm Park

A mostly paved trail circles Kinder Farm Park, a 288–acre working farm with playgrounds, gardens, picnic areas, agricultural exhibits, farm animals, and a visitor center. With so much to offer, this is a great place for children and families.

Distance: 2.6-mile loop

Hiking time: About 1.5 hours

Difficulty: Moderate due to distance

Trail surface: Mostly paved surface, some natural-surface trail offshoots

Best season: Year-round

Other trail users: Bicyclists, runners, skaters, bird-watchers

Canine compatibility: Leashed dogs permitted

Fees and permits: Entrance fee; season pass available for all four paid-entry Anne Arundel County parks

Schedule: 7 a.m. to dusk. Closed Tues. Visitor center hours are Mon, Wed, Thurs, and Fri 9 a.m.–4 p.m. and Sat and Sun 10 a.m.–3 p.m. Closed Thanksgiving and Christmas Day.

Maps: Trail maps available at the entry gatehouse, visitor center, and http://kinderfarmpark.org/images/kinderdis.pdf

Trail contacts: 1001 Kinder Farm Park Rd., Millersville; (410) 222-6115; www.aacounty.org/RecParks/parks/kinderfarm or www.kinderfarmpark.org

Other: Horses permitted on some unpaved trails; catch-and-release fishing in the four ponds within the park

Finding the trailhead: From I-97 take exit 14A to MD 100. Take exit 16A to MD 2 south. Turn right on Jumpers Hole Road and then right on Kinder Farm Park Road. After paying the entrance fee at the gatehouse, pass the playground and continue downhill to park by the second pavilion, called Black Oak, at the bottom lot. The trailhead starts at a sign that reads YOUTH CAMPING AND TRAILER PARKING. If you wish to skip the farm attractions and simply use the perimeter trail, turn on Gali Sanchez Road and take the first left before reaching the gate-house. Free parking is located in the lots with access to the perimeter trail. GPS: N39 06.118'/W76 35.082'

The Hike

The perimeter trail circling this working farm and park is much more than a paved asphalt path. Along the way you'll hike by a bamboo forest, ball fields, a disc golf course, a pond, and a Champion river birch tree, meaning it's one of the tallest trees in the state. The farm was named for the German-born Kinder family, who expanded the initial land into a large-scale agricultural operation. You can learn all about the history of the area by stopping in the visitor center, where you'll view historical exhibits, a slide show, and artifacts and antiques like arrowheads, a hand plow, a grain seed sower, a tobacco press, and a beekeeper's veil. You can view what the land used to look like back in the day and browse the gift shop. The on-site home of the Kinder family is currently being restored to its Depression-era condition and will open to the public as a display house for touring.

On the working farm you'll find goats, cows, sheep, chickens, and turkeys in the spring. February and March are good months to see the "new arrivals" of baby sheep. Other sites on the farm include a blacksmith's forge, tobacco barn with tools and exhibits, and working antique sawmill. Catch-and-release fishing is allowed in the four ponds on-site. On the trail you may see deer, foxes, raccoons, bluebirds, ducks, and geese. Although they are not terribly common, this is one of the few places left in the state where you can see Baltimore oriole birds. Black snakes are, however, common in the area.

From the trailhead you'll cross over the perimeter trail and follow the sign for East-West Boulevard trail. Take the first left turn onto a natural-surface trail. This will take you past Bunks Pond, the bamboo forest, and the record-setting river birch tree. Among the towering bamboo you may briefly feel like you've been transported to the South Pacific. Frogs, crickets, and grasshoppers inhabit this area. Once you get to a grassy open area, you'll take the trail to the left to meet back up with the paved perimeter trail, which you will follow to the right. This takes you past some private homes and the playing fields of the local Green Hornets recreation league. The trail passes a public playground and parking area. At about 2 miles you'll walk over a small wooden bridge just before crossing the entrance road, Kinder Farm Park Road. You should now recognize your surroundings as you continue to circle back to your starting point, passing by the visitor center and heading downhill to Kinder Farm's playground and restrooms and eventually back to the pavilion parking and trailhead.

Miles and Directions

0.0 Begin the trail at the edge of the parking lot where a sign reads youth camping and trailer parking.

0.1 Cross the intersection of the perimeter trail. Take the first left onto a natural wooded path.

0.2 Reach Bunks Pond on the left.

0.4 Look left to see the record-setting birch tree and bamboo forest.

0.5 When the trail opens, cut left to meet up with the perimeter trail.

0.6 Hang a right on the perimeter trail.

1.5 Reach the soccer fields.

1.6 Come to the high school athletic fields.

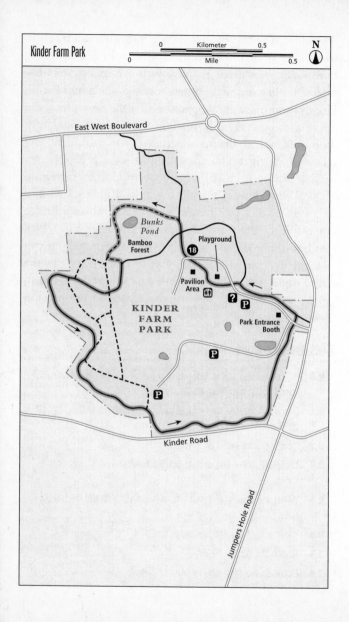

Kinder Farm Park

East West Boulevard

Bunks Pond

Playground

18

Bamboo Forest

Pavilion Area

? P

KINDER FARM PARK

Park Entrance Booth

P

P

Kinder Road

Jumpers Hole Road

Kilometer
0   0.5
Mile
0   0.5

N

1.7 Reach a public playground and parking lot.

1.9 Pass by the Green Hornets baseball field.

2.1 Cross over a wooden bridge.

2.2 Cross over the main entrance road to the park, Kinder Farm Park Road; the entry gatehouse is on your left.

2.3 Pass by the parking and visitor center on your left.

2.5 Pass the Kinder Park playground and restrooms.

2.6 Arrive back at your starting point at the pavilion and parking area at the trailhead.

19 Appalachian Trail: I-70 to Annapolis Rocks

There is a feeling of enchantment when you know you are hiking on a portion of a 2,000-mile trail that extends from Georgia to Maine. Forty-one miles of the Appalachian Trail run through Maryland. This day hike will take you to a typical three-sided shelter and one of the trail's amazing overlooks, Annapolis Rocks, featuring rock formations and scenic views.

Distance: 5.4 miles out and back with spur

Hiking time: About 2.5 hours (but leave plenty of time to linger at the overlook)

Difficulty: Moderate to challenging due to distance and some uphill

Trail surface: Natural

Best season: Year-round

Other trail users: Foot traffic only

Canine compatibility: Leashed dogs permitted

Fees and permits: None required

Schedule: Daily from sunrise to sunset year-round

Maps: Trail map available on the website www.patc.net/Public View/Store/BrowseCategories/ Core/Orders/category.aspx ?catid=5

Trail contacts: 118 Park Street, S.E., Vienna, VA; (703) 242-0315; www.patc.net

Other: Rugged cliffs with steep drop-offs

Finding the trailhead: From I-70 take the Meyersville exit. Turn north onto MD 17, and then turn left on US 40. The parking lot is located just before US 40 crosses over I-70. There is room for twenty to thirty cars in the lot. GPS: N39 32.133'/W77 36.247'

The Hike

Beginning at the parking lot, you'll see a very large sign directing you to the Appalachian Trail. You'll soon come to the bridge over I-70; however, you will not cross over the footbridge. Instead head to the right and continue to parallel the highway until the trail dips into the woods.

The wooded trail is well marked and extremely easy to follow, with white blazes guiding the way. In less than a mile, you will meet up with an intersection with a blue-blazed trail to Pine Knob Shelter. This three-sided structure is typical of AT shelters. Shelters are popular stops for a break or a place to overnight for backpackers and thru-hikers, those out to hike the entire length of the trail from Georgia to Maine. Shelters often have a tent camping area, a privy (bathroom facility), and a water source. Pine Knob Shelter has all of the above facilities. There is a shortcut trail back to the main trail. However, this hike as described takes you back the way you came on the blue-blazed trail to the intersection with the main trail. This time you will continue to head north on the AT toward Annapolis Rocks.

You'll get most of the uphill out of the way in the beginning, and then you have a nice even trail with some downhill the rest of the way to Annapolis Rocks. At about 2.5 miles you'll see a trail sign and blue-blazed trail on the left. Follow this trail past the area caretaker and tent camping area to the famed Annapolis Rocks. The caretaker is typically on-site in the warmer months and helps maintain and monitor the area as well as being a resource for hikers.

Don't be surprised to see lots of folks with their lunch strewn about and rock climbers dangling off the sides of the cliffs. This is one of the most popular rock climbing areas in

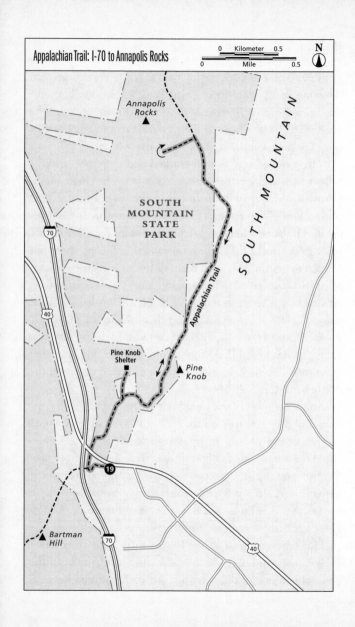

Appalachian Trail: I-70 to Annapolis Rocks

0   Kilometer   0.5
0   Mile   0.5

N

Annapolis Rocks ▲

SOUTH MOUNTAIN

SOUTH MOUNTAIN STATE PARK

Appalachian Trail

Pine Knob Shelter

Pine Knob ▲

I-70

40

19

Bartman Hill ▲

70

40

the state. Off to the west you'll have views of Cumberland Valley and Greenbrier Lake State Park. Keep a lookout for poisonous copperhead snakes tucked away in the rock ledges, as well as eagles, hawks, and deer. You can spend hours here enjoying the views, taking photos, and soaking up the sun on the rocks. Be sure to build in some additional time to do just that!

Miles and Directions

0.0 Start at the parking lot sign that reads Appalachian Trail North and South on a paved path.

0.1 Take the blue-blazed trail to the left. When you reach the bridge over I-70, stay to the right on the trail; do not cross the bridge. Follow the white-blazed trail while paralleling I-70.

0.2 Enter the woods.

0.4 Reach an AT info sign.

0.6 Reach the intersection with a blue-blazed trail to Pine Knob Shelter and the white-blazed Appalachian Trail toward Annapolis Rocks. Follow the blue-blazed trail to the shelter.

0.7 See tent camping sites on your right, followed by the Pine Knob Shelter. Retrace your route back to the AT.

0.8 Turn left and head north on the AT.

1.0 Come to the second intersection with a blue-blazed trail to Pine Knob Shelter.

2.6 Reach the trailhead for Annapolis Rocks; follow the blue blazes to the left toward the rocks and overlook.

2.8 Reach Annapolis Rocks overlook. Turn around and retrace your route along the AT back to the parking lot.

5.4 Arrive back at the trailhead and parking lot.

20 C&O Canal: Angler's Inn to Great Falls

Hike past history as you follow the Chesapeake & Ohio Canal towpath and waterway. Make your way upstream on a flat, wide rail trail for stunning sights of the Potomac River. You'll be rewarded with views of the rapid waters of Great Falls and a museum.

Distance: 4.4 miles out and back with side trail to overlook
Hiking time: About 2 hours
Difficulty: Moderate due to distance
Trail surface: Hard-packed dirt
Best season: Year-round
Other trail users: Bicyclists, trail runners, cross-country skiers
Canine compatibility: Leashed dogs permitted except on the trail to Great Falls Overlook and Billy Goat Trail A.
Fees and permits: Angler's Inn parking area is free. Fees collected at Great Falls Entrance Station only.
Schedule: Open daylight hours year-round; Great Falls Tavern Museum open 9 a.m.–4:30 p.m. daily
Maps: www.nps.gov/choh/ planyourvisit/upload/chohpark map.pdf
Trail contacts: Park Headquarters, 1850 Dual Hwy., Ste. 100, Hagerstown; (301) 739-4200; www.nps.gov/choh/
Other: Replica canal boat rides from Apr to Oct at 11 a.m., 1:30 p.m., and 3 p.m. daily

Finding the trailhead: From I-495 take exit 41 toward Caderock/Great Falls. Merge onto Clara Barton Parkway, and then turn left on MacArthur Boulevard. C&O Canal parking areas are on the left, across from the Old Angler's Inn restaurant. If the parking areas are full, continue to the Great Falls parking area and park for a fee. GPS: N38 58.910'/W77 13.578'

The Hike

While it's a good distance from Baltimore, you can't have a famous trail with falls this stunning within a reasonable driving distance and not include it! While this area is listed in D.C. trail books, Baltimore residents must know that this trail is easily within your reach. The C&O Canal, a national historic park, runs 184.5 miles in total, from Washington, D.C. to Cumberland, Maryland. It was built between 1828 and 1850 and operated until 1924. The C&O Canal began as a passage to the west, operating for nearly one hundred years. It was a necessity for communities along the Potomac River to send coal, lumber, and agricultural products down the waterway to the market.

Today this gem of a trail is a passageway for hikers, bicyclists, and joggers to historical, natural, and recreational opportunities. The section hike mapped here is 4.4 miles out and back and begins from the Angler's Inn parking area. The route described includes a detour that is currently in place. The towpath is closed from milepost 12.4 to 12.7. Therefore, from the parking area you'll first follow the detour trail on the east side of the canal, which parallels the C&O Canal towpath on the opposite side. Note that the trail is a simple-to-follow out-and-back hike and the detour trail closely parallels the actual trail. Therefore, once the detour has been removed, you'll start the trail on the actual towpath and follow the rest of the directions accordingly.

After a little over a mile on the detour route, you'll cross the canal via the bridge on your left and meet up with the towpath. Within steps you'll see the trailhead for the Billy Goat Trail A on your left. This is a very popular trail with great views and a challenging rock scramble. Continue following the towpath, and just before you reach your turnaround point at the Great Falls Tavern, you will come to the sign for an

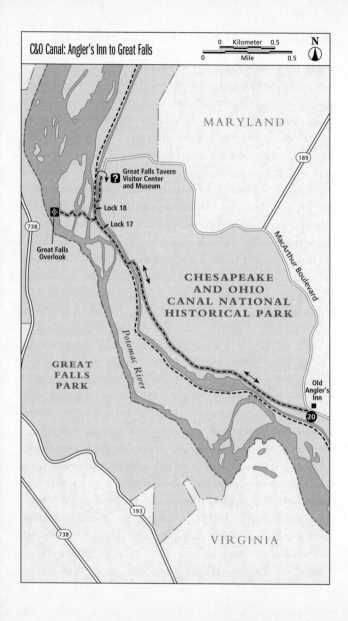

C&O Canal: Angler's Inn to Great Falls

0   Kilometer   0.5

0   Mile   0.5

N

MARYLAND

189

Great Falls Tavern
Visitor Center
and Museum

Lock 18

Lock 17

738

Great Falls
Overlook

CHESAPEAKE
AND OHIO
CANAL NATIONAL
HISTORICAL PARK

MacArthur Boulevard

Potomac River

GREAT
FALLS
PARK

Old
Angler's
Inn

20

193

738

VIRGINIA

overlook, directing you to turn left. Even if you have to fight your way through crowds of people, you do not want to miss the views at this overlook! The boardwalk trail will take you over bridges with several views of the gushing rapids and falls until the trail ends at an observation deck. If you're lucky, you can watch kayakers taking the plunge on some of the most challenging runs around. Once you've snapped lots of pictures, turn around to reconnect with the C&O Canal.

Continue on the towpath in the same direction to reach the Great Falls Tavern Visitor Center and Museum before retracing your steps along the canal to return to the Angler's Inn. The inn is a hot spot for outdoor enthusiasts enjoying a meal on the patio or a celebration drink at the end of an exercise-filled day. So go ahead, reward yourself with a cold beverage. You deserve it!

Miles and Directions

0.0 Begin hiking from the parking lot, following the detour trail.

1.3 Cross the bridge to your left over the canal and head down the stairs on the opposite side to meet up with the towpath trail.

1.4 Pass the trailhead for the Billy Goat Trail A on the left.

1.7 Take the boardwalk trail to the left to reach the Great Falls Overlook.

2.0 Come to the end of the boardwalk and the final overlook of Great Falls. After enjoying the views, return to the overlook trailhead.

2.3 Make a left on the towpath.

2.5 Reach the Great Falls Tavern Visitor Center and Museum. Check out the replica canal boat, and then retrace your steps to your starting point.

4.4 Arrive back at the Angler's Inn parking area.

21 Elk Neck State Park: Lighthouse Trail

An easy trail with open meadows and water views most of the way leads you to the cliffs above the Chesapeake Bay and the Turkey Point Lighthouse at the tip of a peninsula of land between the Elk and Northeast Rivers.

Distance: 2.0-mile lollipop loop
Hiking time: About 1 hour
Difficulty: Easy
Trail surface: Crushed stone, sand, packed dirt
Best season: Year-round
Other trail users: Bicyclists, bird-watchers
Canine compatibility: Leashed dogs permitted
Fees and permits: No fees for this area of the park; donations appreciated

Schedule: Sunrise to sunset. Lighthouse tower open Sat and Sun 10 a.m.–4 p.m. from Easter to mid-Nov. Donations for the lighthouse accepted during these hours.
Maps: Trail map available at park headquarters
Trail contacts: 4395 Turkey Point Rd., North East; (410) 287-5333; www.dnr.state.md.us/publiclands/central/elkneck.asp
Other: Small gift shop located at the lighthouse

Finding the trailhead: Take I-95 to exit 100 onto MD 272. Head south toward North East and follow MD 272 for 14 miles. The road dead-ends in the parking lot for the Lighthouse Trail. GPS: N39 27.587' / W76 00.355'

The Hike

At the parking lot trailhead, you are immediately rewarded with water views from the cliffs above the Chesapeake Bay.

This trail was formerly known as the "blue trail," and you'll see old blue and white blazes on the trees. But you can now follow the well-placed red marker posts on this easy, flat, and wide path that leads you to the Turkey Point Lighthouse and gift shop. One of seven trails in Elk Neck State Park, this is a popular hike, dotted with benches and a couple of picnic tables. The path is made of crushed stone, with a short section of natural packed dirt.

About halfway to the lighthouse, you'll reach the raptor viewing field and an informational kiosk about hawks. Migrating hawks can be seen from September to November, with peak times between 9 a.m. and noon. Seventeen species of raptors have been observed at Turkey Point. The sharp-shinned hawk is the most common. Bald eagles are seen regularly, as well as deer, foxes, and squirrels.

Just before the lighthouse a portable toilet is located on the left. You then approach the 35-foot lighthouse, which is situated on a 100-foot bluff at the confluence of five rivers as they meet the Chesapeake Bay. Sailboats glide through the waters, and picnickers spread out blankets on the lawn for a meal with a view. Walk the forty steps to the top. On a clear day you can see for miles.

The Turkey Point Lighthouse was constructed in 1833 and had more female keepers than any other in Maryland. It's the signature landmark of the park.

In 1925 President Calvin Coolidge appointed Fannie May Salter to the post of lighthouse keeper. She was the only woman lighthouse keeper in America and the last keeper of the Turkey Point Lighthouse. It became automated in 1947. The lighthouse was decommissioned in 2000 and relit in 2002 as a "private aid to navigation." A solar-charged battery now powers it. In season, volunteers stationed at the

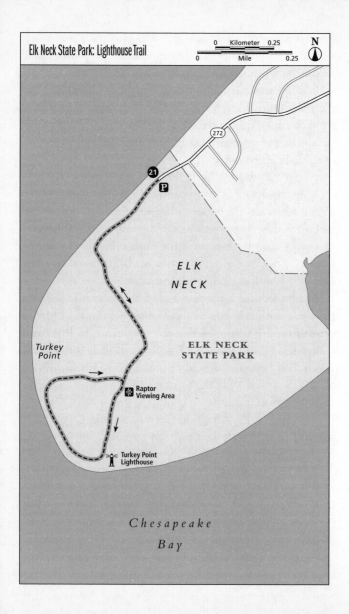

lighthouse are happy to answer questions and share some history with visitors.

This hike is one of the farthest from Baltimore listed in this guidebook. However, the lighthouse destination combined with an easy path and great views of the famed Chesapeake Bay make for an ideal hike for families with children that is worth the drive.

Miles and Directions

0.0 Begin your hike at the parking lot. As you start on the trail, cliffs and views of the bay will be on your right.

0.7 Reach the raptor viewing field and information kiosk with information about hawks.

0.8 Reach the Turkey Point Lighthouse and gift shop. After your visit, head to the right, after you reach the water, and hug the water's edge, until the trail dips back under tree cover.

0.9 Follow the blue/white trail markers onto a packed-dirt trail that leads into the trees.

1.0 Stay on the trail as it bears to the right.

1.1 The trail bears to the right once again.

1.3 Meet up with the trail you walked in on, and turn left to retrace your route back to the parking lot.

2.0 Arrive back at the trailhead and parking lot.

Area Clubs and Trail Groups

Mountain Club of Maryland

7923 Galloping Circle, Baltimore; (410) 377-6266; www
.mcomd.org

Founded in 1934, Mountain Club of Maryland is the oldest and
the premier hiking group in the state. The club is a Baltimore-
based volunteer organization centered on hiking. It leads hikes,
camping trips, canoeing outings, and other outdoor activities in
addition to maintaining sections of the Appalachian Trail.

Maryland Outdoor Club

www.marylandoutdoorclub.org

This 100 percent volunteer-run organization hosts all types
of outdoor activities oriented toward young professionals
in the Baltimore and Washington, D.C., area, but is open to
anyone. Take part in outings like hiking, biking, backpacking,
rafting, and camping.

Baltimore Outdoor Sierrans, Greater Baltimore Group, Maryland Chapter, Sierra Club

http://maryland.sierraclub.org/baltimore/bos

The Baltimore Outdoor Sierrans hosts socials and outings for
young people, generally between the ages of 25 and 45, inter-
ested in enjoying the outdoors and having a positive impact
on the environment. Sierra Club membership is not required.

Meetup Groups

www.meetup.com

Search "hiking" and "Baltimore" to find a plethora of hiking
and outdoor groups, each tailored to a specific niche. Here
you can find groups geared toward hiking with dogs or hiking
in a particular area of Maryland, entrepreneurs who are also
outdoor enthusiasts, and groups specific to age and experience.

About the Author

Heather Sanders Connellee was born and raised in Baltimore. Since the age of 14, she has been exploring the trails in and around her native city. Her wanderlust and love of the outdoors have taken her to hiking trails across the country and around the world. She spent six months backpacking the Appalachian Trail from Georgia to Maine. Heather is the former trail programs manager for the American Hiking Society, where she spearheaded National Trails Day and the National Trails Fund and led various volunteer trail groups. Heather is editor of *American Hiker* magazine and writes for numerous outdoor and travel publications. She enjoys hiking, backpacking, rock climbing, kayaking, biking, and anything and everything outdoors.

Heather and her husband Grant along with two dogs and a cat recently moved to Harford County, Maryland. Their bucket list is longer than the Mississippi River and includes thru-hiking the Pacific Crest Trail, summiting Mt. Kilimanjaro, and bagging all forty-six of the Adirondack High Peaks. Heather currently holds the position of Vice President, Marketing & Development at Leffler Agency, Inc., a Baltimore-based advertising firm. Heather's heart is in the mountains, and home will always be Baltimore.